KETO

Desserts™

Your Guide to Keto Baking

Kelley Herring

Recipes

ICE CREAMS

FROSTINGS & TOPPINGS

A Personal Note
FROM THE AUTHOR OF KETO DESSERTS

Every few years a new diet trend catches the attention of the masses.

In recent years, the "Paleo Diet" and "Gluten Free" have enjoyed their time in the spotlight – and for good reason! Millions of people worldwide have experienced better health and faster fat loss by following a grain-free, ancestral diet. However, a new way of eating has taken the spotlight – the **Ketogenic Diet.**

The Keto Diet is:

- Rich in healthy fats

- Moderate in protein, and

- Low in carbohydrates.

Limiting carbohydrates – while increasing healthy dietary fat – helps to reprogram your metabolism to its factory setting. It causes you to enter a metabolic state, known as **ketosis**, where your body uses stored fat and compounds called "ketones" for energy.

In other words, your metabolism shifts from burning carbohydrates (and storing the excess as flabby fat) to burning unsightly fat and using it to fuel your daily life. And when you are in "ketosis" you will continue burning fat, even when you're sitting down doing nothing.

This **metabolic reprogramming – from sugar burner to fat burner** – is what makes the ketogenic diet so powerful for weight loss!

And once you reach this state of hormonal balance, your energy and mental clarity soar, as hunger and cravings fade away. In fact, one of the most widely reported benefits of the keto diet is that it helps people go for extended periods without eating – while still feeling happy, energized and fully satisfied. No wonder it has become so popular!

But the truth is...

DESPITE SURGING POPULARITY THERE IS NOTHING "NEW" ABOUT THE KETO DIET

The metabolic state of "ketosis" is a natural evolutionary advantage. It is what allowed our hunter-gatherer ancestors to remain mentally sharp and energetic, even when food was scarce. And considering that sugar and carbohydrate-rich foods were limited, our ancient ancestors naturally spent most of their time in a ketogenic state.

> *"When the brain is powered by ketones, it functions a lot better. This allows us to remain clever, even when calorie-deprived, like in our hunter-gatherer days."*
>
> Dr. David Perlmutter, M.D.
> Author, *Grain Brain*

In other words, the keto diet is the true "Paleo Diet". It is the way of eating on which our brains and bodies evolved to function best. It is no exaggeration to say that without our ability to function in a state of ketosis, the human species would not have survived.

In the modern era, the ketogenic diet has been used to successfully treat epilepsy for more than 100 years. And to this day, it remains one of the most effective ways to reduce the incidence and severity of seizures – helping children and adults worldwide to reduce or discontinue medication and end their suffering for good![1]

But these are not the only advantages that help to explain the new popularity of this old way of eating...

THE KETOGENIC DIET:
ANTI-CANCER, BRAIN-BOOSTING & BLOOD SUGAR BENEFITS

Over the last several decades, hundreds of peer-reviewed studies have proven that a diet rich in healthy fats and low in carbohydrates provides major health benefits – including the opportunity for you to enjoy a much longer **healthy lifespan**.

The *PURE Study*, published in *The Lancet*, found that high-carb diets are linked to early death... while diets rich in healthy fats are associated with healthy longevity.[2]

Another major benefit of the ketogenic diet is its ability to **starve cancer cells**. Healthy cells can easily adapt from using glucose to using ketones. In fact, healthy cells *thrive* on ketones! Cancer cells, however, lack this metabolic flexibility. Mutated cells are crippled and destroyed in the absence of glucose – making the ketogenic diet one of the most powerful and effective dietary therapies for the prevention and treatment of cancer.[3]

Ketones are also **miraculous for your brain**. Studies show the keto diet can improve cognitive function and help some patients with Alzheimer's, Parkinson's, ALS and other neurological conditions to recover.[4] So it is no surprise that a Mayo Clinic study, published in *The Journal of Alzheimer's Disease*, found that people on a high-fat diet had a 44 percent *reduced* risk for dementia, while those on a high-carb diet had an 89 percent *increased* risk![5]

And let's not forget about the **epidemics of type 2 diabetes, pre-diabetes** and **metabolic syndrome**, which affect more than 100 million Americans – or nearly one-third of the population![6] The great news is that these deadly chronic conditions can be **reversed with tremendous success** – and *without* the use of toxic drugs!

The key is a combination of exercise and the right diet. And when it comes to restoring your hormonal balance and maintaining healthy blood sugar levels, no dietary strategy is more effective than one rich in healthy fats, moderate in protein and low in carbohydrates.

Considering these life-changing benefits, you might be asking...

WHAT ARE THE DRAWBACKS TO KETO?

There is debate that a _very_ low carb diet can be problematic for some people with pre-existing thyroid conditions. For the vast majority of us, however, there are no health risks to following a ketogenic diet. There are only benefits.

But that does not mean it's always easy. There can be some drawbacks…

If you don't know what kind of meals to make, it can be difficult to sustain a keto diet. Many people struggle with the effort of planning and preparing food. Not to mention the time and knowledge required to keep track of your net carbs and macronutrient ratios! And if you don't include enough variety, your ketogenic diet could be deficient in important micronutrients.

Then there are the meal plans and recipe books that add gobs of fat and dairy to every recipe – and magically call it "keto". Many of these gimmick programs are not ketogenic at all, leading users to become discouraged when they don't experience the results they expect.

But perhaps the most common complaint about keto – and the reason why many people try and then fail – is that they simply do not want to give up their favorite comfort foods. Or they cut back on these foods for a while and then "fall off the wagon" under the temptation of bread, pizza, pancakes… and sweet, decadent, delicious desserts.

I certainly understand this dilemma. It is the reason you are holding this book in your hands today. And the great news is…

YOU CAN STILL ENJOY ALL OF YOUR FAVORITE COMFORT FOODS ON THE KETO DIET!

There's a comforting nostalgia attached to the foods you grew up enjoying. That's why the smell of fresh bread baking in the oven or chocolate chip cookies cooling on the counter can instantly transport your mind to Grandma's kitchen… decades in the past.

Many of our favorite comfort foods also involve positive celebrations. Birthdays, weddings, anniversaries and holidays are all centered on the enjoyment of food and connection with ones we love. The very acts of preparing, eating and sharing these foods can be a form of therapy in itself.

It is said that cooking and baking provide food for the body – and medicine for the soul.

So, while it's true that nothing is more important than your health, it would be a shame if you had to give up the enjoyment of your favorite foods and miss out on these simple (and delicious) pleasures.

So, let me show you how you really can have your cake... AND be well too!™

KETO DESSERTS: HOW IT ALL BEGAN...

The recipes in this book represent more than 20 years of dedicated research. It all began when I became very sick at the age of 18, while studying to become a medical doctor.

During my sophomore year in college, a dismal cloud of sickness came over me. What began as a sore throat, progressed to open sores trailing down my esophagus. I had to use a toxic numbing spray to eat without tears. My digestive system was constantly distressed. The slightest colds turned into weeks of illness. And crushing fatigue made it hard to even rise from bed... not to mention, keeping up with a rigorous biology and chemistry curriculum.

And these symptoms persisted for years...

My despair intensified as doctor after doctor sent me away with another diagnosis, another specialist to see, and another prescription. But you know the one thing, not one of those dozen doctors ever asked? They didn't ask me about my diet. They didn't ask what I was putting in my body. And they didn't test me for food allergies or intolerances.

After exhausting my options, I knew I could only count on myself for healing. I took a much deeper look at the foods I was eating. And I began to study the great body of scientific literature on human health and nutritional healing.

I STUDIED THE SCIENCE OF NUTRITION...
AS IF MY LIFE DEPENDED ON IT

Around this time, I began to follow a *very* strict elimination diet. It wasn't fun. But within days, my throat began to heal. I soon regained my energy. My digestive system normalized. And it wasn't long before I charted a course back to health. All it took was a few changes to my diet!

Later, a naturopathic doctor gave me a range of tests. He helped me discover I had multiple food allergies and sensitivities (including gluten). I learned that some of these foods had caused me to develop a leaky gut. And this led to an autoimmune condition, where my immune system attacked my own body – hence the unrelenting sores in my throat.

I was thrilled to have my health and energy back. But I was also disillusioned with "modern" medicine. To be honest, I was angry about what happened to me. I didn't expect my doctors to have _all_ the answers. But they hardly looked for any answers! They wanted to write a quick prescription and send me on my way.

I still graduated with degrees in biology and chemistry. But I no longer wanted to be a doctor. I wanted to help people understand their health – so they would never _need_ a doctor. I wanted to help people prevent the devastating chronic diseases caused by the foods we eat.

In the midst of my own life and death struggle...

I DISCOVERED THE TRUE PURPOSE FOR MY LIFE

I didn't want anyone to endure the misery and emotional uncertainty I experienced (especially when the remedy can often be found in a few simple dietary changes). I was also highly motivated to reinvent my favorite comfort foods, because my own diet was so restrictive at the time.

I wanted to enjoy those delicious foods again – without worrying about my health or my waistline!

Twenty years ago, I dedicated my life to studying the impact of the foods we eat on our long-term health. Two goals became the focus of my career and driving ambitions in my life. I set out to:

1. **Learn** (and then **educate**) about the power of foods to promote health and protect against disease.

2. **Discover** (and then **teach**) how to enjoy ALL your favorite foods – 100 percent guilt free!

My youthful enthusiasm must have been persuasive, as my first accomplishment was to secure a partnership with McGraw Hill, one of the largest publishers in the world. I'll never forget the butterflies I felt, when the executives reached across the table to shake my hand... and offered to publish a series of four books produced by my company, Healing Gourmet!

I quickly recruited a team of doctors and nutritionists from some of the world's leading universities – and a team of chefs from Johnson & Wales. In one year, we produced all four books! And they were a big success – translated into half a dozen languages. But it was McGraw Hill that enjoyed the success!

Due to my youthful innocence at the conference table, my earnings for those _four_ books were less than I would have made waiting tables. But I wouldn't trade the experience for the world! I was thrilled to combine my passion for health research with my love of recipe creation.

I continued to focus on my two primary goals, and set out to...

REINVENT THE WORLD'S MOST CLASSIC COMFORT FOODS

As a nutritional biochemist, I've spent a lot of time in the library – and the laboratory. But my true passion has always been cooking and baking and creating recipes. It is the "kitchen laboratory" where my heart is truly at home.

When I began to craft these recipes, most people had never even heard the term "gluten free." There were no grain-free, all-natural, low-glycemic baking mixes on store shelves. There weren't even any recipe books that used the ingredients I was working with.

Every recipe we developed was a matter of experimentation, documentation... and often weeks of trial and error. You see, baking is a science. And baking with gluten-free, low-glycemic ingredients is an _exact_ science.

Changing a single ingredient – or the ratio of ingredients to one another – can turn something delicious into a disaster. And I wasn't just changing one ingredient. Sometimes I was replacing them all!

Eventually the hard work and experiments paid off. Over the years, I discovered the secrets to using **grain-free flours**... **healthy, slimming fats**... binders... leaveners... and **natural, keto-friendly sweeteners**... until I could finally create predictably delicious results, every time.

I learned how to use **functional ingredients** and **metabolic power foods** to precisely match the taste, texture, rise, flavor and sweetness of all your favorite comfort foods – from cakes, cheesecakes and cookies, to crackers, muffins, biscuits, brownies, pancakes, waffles, bread, biscotti and more!

And I'm not talking about second-rate imitations. I'm talking about all the decadence you crave – _without_ the guilt and harmful ingredients. I'm talking about good-for-you versions of these foods, so delicious you'd swear they're bad for you!

In 2007, Healing Gourmet published the first of these recipes and our nutritional research in a series of books, starting with **Guilt-Free Desserts** and then **Better Breads**. These books became an instant sensation, as hundreds of thousands of people worldwide discovered you really can have your cake... AND be well too.™

But we never stopped making those recipes better. We continued to select the best of the best, tweaking, improving and taking beautiful pictures of our creations along the way. **Keto Desserts** is the result of this gradual, continual and relentless improvement. The recipes in this book are truly...

THE PINNACLE OF HEALTHY DESSERTS

The great news is that you do not have to choose between the enjoyment of desserts and being healthy. You just need to choose healthy desserts. And that is exactly what you're holding in your hands today!

In the pages that follow, you will find nourishing and healthy makeovers of all the mouth-watering desserts you know and love. Each recipe has been tested dozens of times, to ensure it is easy to make and that _your_ results will be as beautiful and delicious as those pictured.

Every one of these sweet and delicious desserts is **very low sugar**... **rich in healthy fats**... **grain and gluten free**... and **meets the "Magic Macros" of the ketogenic diet**! In other words, these desserts can actually help you sculpt a lean physique – instead of puffing up your muffin top!

I sincerely hope you enjoy these classic desserts as much as we have enjoyed creating them for you. We hope that baking these creations will bring you joy – and get you closer to the body and health you deserve!

Have Your Cake... AND Be Well Too!

Kelley Herring
Founder, Healing Gourmet

1. Stafstrom C, Rho J. The Ketogenic Diet as a Treatment Paradigm for Diverse Neurological Disorders. *Front Pharmacol.* 2012; 3: 59.
2. Dehghan M, Dia, R, et al. Associations of fats and carbohydrate intake with cardiovascular disease and mortality in 18 countries from five continents (PURE): a prospective cohort study. *Lancet.* 2017;390(10107):2050-2062.
3. Vander Heiden M, Cantley C, Thompson B. Understanding the Warburg Effect: The Metabolic Requirements of Cell Proliferation. *Science.* 2009;324(5930):1029-1033.
4. Gasior M, Rogawski M, Hartmana A. Neuroprotective and disease-modifying effects of the ketogenic diet. *Behav Pharmacol.* 2006; 17(5-6): 431–439.
5. Roberts R, et al. Relative intake of macronutrients impacts risk of mild cognitive impairment or dementia. *J Alzheimers Dis.* 2012; 32: (2)329-39.
6. Centers for Disease Control and Prevention. (2012). New CDC report: More than 100 million Americans have diabetes or prediabetes. Retrieved August 31, 2018 from https://www.cdc.gov/media/releases/2017/p0718-diabetes-report.html

The Keto Solution™

30-Day Fast-Track System for a Better Body & Sharper Brain

Discover How You Can Easily Follow a
100% Ketogenic Diet While Still Enjoying
<u>ALL the Foods You Love</u>
(And Spending 70% Less Time in the Kitchen)!

www.KETOSOLUTION.net

Do You Love Bread, Pizza, Pancakes, Waffles, Cookies & Dessert...

But Not the Time and Effort it Takes to Buy Ingredients & Bake Recipes from Scratch?

WELLNESS BAKERIES HAS THE SOLUTION!

Learn More about our Delicious
Keto & Paleo-Friendly Baking Mixes...

**Enter Coupon Code KETO for
10% off Your First Order!**

www.WELLNESSBAKERIES.com

Before You Bake:
A FEW REMINDERS

Few things in the kitchen are worse than spending your time and money to make a recipe that flops. We don't want that to happen to you! Baking should be fun and rewarding. So we have taken great care to make the instructions for the recipes in this book simple and clear – and the preparations as easy as possible.

You should be able to whip up most of these treats in 15 to 30 minutes (active time). And you won't need any fancy equipment or complicated techniques. We worked hard to make every recipe foolproof – even for the most novice baker!

Most important, we taste tested every recipe over and over until it was just right. So not only can you bake these desserts with confidence that your results will come out just like the pictures... you can also be sure that you and your family will _love_ every one of these delicious creations!

But there are some important tips that will make your job easier in the kitchen. So please take a few minutes to read these reminders before you set out on your **Keto Desserts** baking adventure!

INGREDIENTS & SUPPLIES

Most of these recipes require basic tools you should already have in your kitchen – like mixing bowls, a hand mixer, cookie sheets and baking pans. But there are a handful of recipes that call for specialized tools, such as mini tart pans or a spring-form pan to make a cheesecake.

Likewise, many of the ingredients you need are also probably already in your kitchen. And those you do not have, are easy to find in any well-stocked grocery store. If your local grocery store doesn't carry an ingredient, check the health food store. And of course, every ingredient can easily be found on Amazon.

To keep it simple, we created a page where you can find all the ingredients and supplies you need. If you're not sure which pan to use or you don't know which brand of ingredient might be preferred, check out our top recommendations here: **KetoDesserts.net/Resources**

SWEET SYNERGY: JUST LIKE SUGAR & BETTER FOR YOUR HEALTH

Sugar adds more than sweetness to desserts. It provides bulk and helps to retain moisture. It acts as a preservative. And it also caramelizes, helping to provide a crisp texture and pleasant chew. Of course, you also know that too much sugar can destroy your health!

That's why, here at Healing Gourmet, we have spent more than a decade researching and testing all-natural, low-glycemic sweeteners. Our goal was to help you achieve the "sugary" results you desire in your desserts – without the guilt and harmful effects of sugar.

Most of the desserts in this book use a combination **erythritol** and **stevia** – two natural sweeteners that boast zero calories and zero glycemic index. The sweet combination of these two ingredients produces results that taste – and bake – just like sugar!

If you're not familiar with erythritol, just know that your body already is. Unlike dangerous artificial sweeteners, this naturally-occurring sugar alcohol is found in a variety of foods, including watermelon, pears and grapes, as well as fermented foods like sake, wine and soy sauce.

And numerous peer-reviewed studies now prove that erythritol is not only safe – it can be truly beneficial! If you're interested to learn more about the benefits and properties of this natural sweetener – and why we choose it for the dessert recipes in this book – please visit: **KetoDesserts.net/Sweetener**

WHY (AND HOW) TO POWDER ERYTHRITOL?

Erythritol is a granular sweetener, just like sugar. And that's fine in a recipe that requires baking or when it is mixed with a liquid. In that case, the granules dissolve and the sweetener is easily incorporated.

But in some recipes – like a whipped frosting – the granules won't dissolve. If you don't powder the erythritol first, you might be left with a "gritty" result. So, while this step is not required, it will produce the best results. Powdered erythritol can also be used as "powdered sugar" to sprinkle as a garnish on top of your desserts.

We prefer a Magic Bullet mini-blender for this purpose. But you can also use a coffee grinder, full-size blender, food processor or even a mortar and pestle. In each recipe where it is helpful to powder this ingredient, it is clearly noted.

STEVIA: ALWAYS SWEETEN "TO TASTE"

Each one of us has our own perception of sweetness. What is "just right" for one person, might be way too sweet for you. If you have been eating a high-sugar diet for years – and then switch to a ketogenic diet – you may also notice that your perception of sweetness changes over time.

In addition to your personal perception, when it comes to stevia in particular, there can be huge variations in the level of sweetness from one brand to the next. And considering stevia is 200 to 300 times sweeter than sugar – even a tiny bit too much can ruin a recipe.

Whenever you see stevia in the recipes below, you will also see the recommendation, "to taste". That means you should first add _less_ than the amount called for. Mix it in and taste the results with a spoon. If you prefer it a bit sweeter, add a little more and taste again. Do this until the sweetness is just right... for you!

We do not recommend that you change the amount of erythritol specified. This ingredient is only 70 percent as sweet as sugar, so it is much more forgiving. More importantly, these recipes have been tested many times to include just the right amount of this ingredient.

MEASUREMENTS: CUPS VS. GRAMS?

Baking is a science. For many of us, our first chemistry lessons happened in the kitchen – standing beside our mother or grandmother as she explained why bread rises, how white sugar turns to brown caramel, or why the properties of eggs help bind ingredients together.

And just like the chemistry lab, one tiny change to a formula can make a big difference in the results. Thankfully, these dessert recipes are not as exacting as bread recipes can be. But accurate measurements are still important.

So you will notice that we often provide gram weights for dry ingredients. These are the _exact_ measurements we used in our test kitchen. Of course, we still provide volume measurements and you can use cups and tablespoons, if you prefer.

Just realize that these measurements are not going to be as accurate. For example, one "cup" of almond flour (lightly scooped) might weigh 80 grams. Another cup of almond flour (densely packed) could weigh 120 grams. That's a significant difference – and the reason why we provide exact gram weights.

If you don't have a kitchen scale, you certainly don't need one. But it can be a very helpful and inexpensive tool that may save you time and trouble.

STORING & SERVING

Most of these desserts will easily last a week or more, stored in an airtight container in the refrigerator. They can also be frozen indefinitely and served later. If you do wish to freeze these treats, we recommend slicing the dessert into individual portions first. Then wrap each portion in plastic wrap. And store the individually-wrapped servings in a freezer bag.

If you find that these desserts have dried out a bit after a few days, there is a simple and effective solution. Put the dessert in the microwave and reheat in 10 second bursts. Check after each burst and take it out when it has just begun to soften and warm. We generally don't like to use a microwave. But this "10-second trick" can be really helpful and can turn a five-day old stale cookie into a warm, soft delight.

So, that's all the tips, tricks and reminders we have. Now it's time for baking!

Cheesecakes

KETO NY-STYLE CHEESECAKE

This rich and creamy, NY-style cheesecake will please even the most devout fans of classic cheesecake!

YIELD: One 7" cake (12 servings)

CRUST INGREDIENTS

- 1 cup blanched almond flour (100 g)
- ¼ cup grass-fed butter (melted)

FILLING INGREDIENTS

- 16 ounces organic whole cream cheese
- ¾ cup organic whole sour cream
- 3 large pastured eggs
- ¾ cup erythritol (150 g)
- 35 drops liquid stevia
- ½ tsp. lemon zest
- 1 tsp. vanilla extract

DIRECTIONS

1. Preheat oven to 325 F. Line the bottom and sides of a 7" cheesecake pan with parchment paper. Bring all ingredients to room temperature.

2. Combine the crust ingredients, mixing well. Press into the lined pan, packing tightly. Poke the bottom of the crust with a fork to make small holes.

3. Transfer to preheated oven and bake 10 minutes. Then remove and let cool.

4. Meanwhile, in a large deep bowl add the cream cheese, sour cream, eggs, erythritol, stevia, vanilla and lemon zest. Beat with an electric mixer until completely smooth.

5. Scrape batter into par-baked crust. Tap pan on the counter to remove bubbles and allow filling to settle.

6. Make a water bath. Wrap the bottom of the cheesecake pan tightly with heavy aluminum foil. This prevents water from entering the cheesecake during baking, so take your time. Place wrapped cheesecake pan into a larger pan. Add water to about 1½ inches up the side of the pan.

7. Transfer to oven and bake 55-70 minutes. The center should be slightly jiggly after baking. It will set as it cools. Cool on a wire rack for 30 minutes. Chill in the refrigerator for another hour (or preferably overnight).

NUTRITION INFORMATION

256 calories, 24 g fat, 12 g saturated fat, 8 g monounsaturated fat, 2 g polyunsaturated fat, 109 mg cholesterol, 16 g carbohydrate, 3 g NET carbs, 8 g sugar alcohols, 2 g sugar, 3 g fiber, 7 g protein,159 mg potassium, 119 mg phosphorous, 166 mg sodium, 30 mg magnesium

MACRONUTRIENT RATIO

85% FAT ■ 11% PROTEIN ■ 5% CARBOHYDRATE

KETO CHOCOLATE CHEESECAKE

If you're looking for a rich and decadent dessert, this classic chocolate cheesecake (made keto) fits the bill! For a unique twist or holiday rendition, add peppermint or almond extract.

YIELD: One 7" cake (12 servings)

CRUST INGREDIENTS

- 1 cup blanched almond flour (100 g)
- 3 Tbsp. grass-fed butter(melted)
- 1 Tbsp. cocoa powder
- Pinch sea salt
- 10 drops liquid stevia

FILLING INGREDIENTS

- 16 ounces organic whole cream cheese
- 2 large pastured eggs
- ⅔ cup erythritol, powdered (130 g)
- 3½ ounces Lily's Dark Chocolate Chips (melted)
- 30 drops liquid stevia
- 3 Tbsp. organic cocoa powder
- 1 tsp. vanilla extract

DIRECTIONS

1. Preheat oven to 350 F. Line the bottom of a 7" cheesecake pan with unbleached parchment paper. Bring all ingredients to room temperature.

2. In a small bowl, combine crust ingredients. Mix well to form dough, which holds together when pinched. If not, add melted butter by the teaspoon.

3. Press dough tightly into bottom of the lined pan. Poke the crust with a fork to make small holes. Transfer to oven to par-bake for 10 minutes.

4. While crust is baking, make the filling. In a medium bowl, add the eggs and softened cream cheese. Beat with an electric mixer on medium-low until free of lumps. Add the melted chocolate, 3 Tbsp. cocoa powder, vanilla and remaining stevia (to taste). Beat on high to fully incorporate.

5. Scrape batter into par-baked crust. Tap pan on the counter to settle filling and remove bubbles.

6. Make a water bath. Wrap the bottom of the cheesecake pan tightly with heavy aluminum foil. [This prevents water from entering the cheesecake during baking, so take your time.] Place the wrapped cheesecake pan into a larger pan. Add water to about 1½ inches up the side of the pan.

7. Transfer to oven and bake 45-60 minutes. The center should be slightly jiggly after baking.

8. Remove from oven. Cool in the water bath for 30 minutes. Remove cheesecake from water bath and cool on the counter for an hour. Cover with plastic wrap and chill overnight in the refrigerator.

9. Garnish with a mint sprig, blackberry and melted chocolate chips, if desired.

NUTRITION INFORMATION

257 calories, 24 g fat, 12 g saturated fat, 8 g monounsaturated fat, 2 g polyunsaturated fat, 83 mg cholesterol, 19 g carbohydrate, 3 g NET carbs, 12 g sugar alcohols, 0.6 g sugar, 4 g fiber, 7 g protein,148 mg potassium, 113 mg phosphorous, 142 mg sodium, 37 mg magnesium

MACRONUTRIENT RATIO

84% FAT ■ 11% PROTEIN ■ 5% CARBOHYDRATE

KETO STRAWBERRY-LIME "CHEESE" CAKE

This berry-infused vegan cheesecake is creamy, sweet and tangy... and makes the perfect ending to a summer meal.

YIELD: One 7" cake (16 servings)

CRUST INGREDIENTS

- 1 cup blanched almond flour (100 g)
- ¼ cup virgin coconut oil (melted)
- ½ tsp. sea salt

FILLING INGREDIENTS

- 4 Tbsp. cacao butter (melted)
- 5 Tbsp. virgin coconut oil (melted)
- 7 ounces raw macadamia nuts, soaked overnight, drained and rinsed
- ½ cup coconut milk
- ½ cup lime juice
- 2 cups halved organic strawberries
- ½ cup erythritol, powdered (100 g)
- 20 drops liquid stevia

DIRECTIONS

1. Preheat oven to 350 F. Line the bottom only of a 7" spring-form cheesecake pan with unbleached parchment paper. Powder the erythritol.

2. In a small bowl, combine the crust ingredients. Mix well to form dough which holds together when pinched. If not, add melted oil by the teaspoon.

3. Press dough tightly into the bottom of the lined pan. Poke with a fork to make small holes. Transfer to the oven to par-bake for 10-12 minutes. Let cool completely.

4. While crust is cooling, make the filling. In a blender, add the melted coconut oil and cacao butter, soaked macadamia nuts, coconut milk, strawberries, lime juice, stevia and erythritol. Blend on high until a smooth, uniform consistency is achieved.

5. Scrape filling into par-baked crust. Tap on counter to settle filling. Cover loosely with plastic wrap and refrigerate until set (about 8 hours). You may also freeze for 1-2 hours.

6. Once set, run a butter knife around the outside edge. Unlatch the spring form to unmold. Slice and serve.

NUTRITION INFORMATION

250 calories, 26 g fat, 12 g saturated fat, 10 g monounsaturated fat, 1 g polyunsaturated fat, 0 mg cholesterol, 12 g carbohydrate, 3 g NET carbs, 6 g sugar alcohols, 2 g sugar, 2 g fiber, 3 g protein, 150 mg potassium, 70 mg phosphorous, 38 mg sodium, 41 mg magnesium

MACRONUTRIENT RATIO

91% FAT ■ 4% PROTEIN ■ 5% CARBOHYDRATE

KETO TRUFFLE "CHEESE" CAKE

This uber-rich truffle cheesecake is the most decadent of the keto cheesecake recipes in this series. Serve a thin slice with a dollop of fresh whipped cream and dark chocolate shavings or cinnamon.

YIELD: One 7" cake (16 servings)

CRUST INGREDIENTS

- 1 cup blanched almond flour (100 g)
- 3 Tbsp. coconut oil (melted)
- Pinch sea salt
- 2 Tbsp. cocoa powder
- 1 Tbsp. coconut milk

FILLING INGREDIENTS

- 7 ounces raw macadamia nuts. Soaked overnight, rinsed and drained
- 4 Tbsp. raw cacao butter (melted)
- 3 Tbsp. virgin coconut oil (melted)
- 2 ounces baking chocolate (melted)
- 40 drops liquid stevia (to taste)
- ⅔ cup erythritol, powdered (130 g)
- 1 tsp. vanilla extract
- ½ cup cocoa powder (50g)
- ½ cup coconut milk
- ¼ tsp. sea salt

DIRECTIONS

1. Preheat oven to 350 F. Line the bottom only of a 7" spring-form cheesecake pan with unbleached parchment paper.

2. In a small bowl, combine crust ingredients. Mix well to form dough, which holds together when pinched. If not, add melted oil by the teaspoon.

3. Press dough tightly into the bottom of the lined pan. Poke with a fork to make small holes. Transfer to the oven to par-bake for 10-12 minutes. Let cool completely.

4. While crust is cooling, make the filling. In a blender, add cheesecake filling ingredients. Blend on high until a smooth, uniform consistency is achieved.

5. Scrape filling into par-baked crust. Tap on the counter to settle filling. Cover loosely with plastic wrap and refrigerate until set (about 8 hours). You may also freeze for 2-3 hours and then defrost before cutting.

6. Once set, run a butter knife around the outside edge, then unlatch the spring form.

7. Serve with fresh whipped cream and garnish with chocolate shavings or cinnamon, if desired.

NUTRITION INFORMATION

245 calories, 25 g fat, 11 g saturated fat, 10 g monounsaturated fat, 1 g polyunsaturated fat, 0 mg cholesterol, 13 g carbohydrate, 3 g NET carbs, 8 g sugar alcohols, 2 g sugar, 3 g fiber, 4 g protein,190 mg potassium, 101 mg phosphorous, 39 mg sodium, 65 mg magnesium

MACRONUTRIENT RATIO

90% FAT ■ 6% PROTEIN ■ 4% CARBOHYDRATE

KETO PUMPKIN "CHEESE" CAKE

This grain- and dairy-free cheesecake brings flavors of Fall together with a creamy, pumpkin-rich base for a satisfying treat. Don't forget the whipped cream!

YIELD: One 9" cake (24 servings)

CRUST INGREDIENTS

- 1⅓ cups blanched almond flour (135 g)
- 1 cup pecans (100 g)
- 6 Tbsp. grass-fed butter or coconut oil (melted)
- 1 Tbsp. erythritol, powdered
- 2 tsp. vanilla extract
- ½ tsp. sea salt

FILLING INGREDIENTS

- 5 large pastured eggs
- 1½ cups pumpkin puree (250 g)
- 2 cups raw macadamia nuts, soaked overnight, drained and rinsed (250 g)
- 1 cup coconut milk
- ⅔ cup coconut oil (melted)
- 1 Tbsp. arrowroot or potato starch
- 1 Tbsp. organic apple cider vinegar
- 2 tsp. grass-fed gelatin
- 30 drops liquid stevia (to taste)
- 3 Tbsp. spiced rum
- ¾ cup erythritol, powdered (150 g)
- 1 Tbsp. vanilla extract
- 2 tsp. cinnamon
- ½ tsp. ginger powder
- ½ tsp. nutmeg

DIRECTIONS

1. Preheat oven to 325 F. Grease the bottom and sides of a 9" spring form pan. Line the bottom with unbleached parchment paper.

2. Make the crust. Add all crust ingredients to a food processor. Pulse until the dough comes together.

3. Press crust evenly into the lined pan. Transfer to oven and bake for 10 minutes. Remove and let crust cool. Turn the oven down to 250 F.

4. Make the filling. Add the soaked nuts, coconut milk and eggs to a blender. Blend for 45 seconds. Add remaining filling ingredients and blend until silky smooth.

5. Pour filling into crust, smoothing the top. Bake for 1½ hours. Let cool for an hour, then refrigerate overnight.

6. Drizzle with **Low Carb Caramel** *(page 128)* and toasted pecans or serve with a dollop of fresh whipped cream or **Whipped Coconut Cream** *(page 140)*.

NUTRITION INFORMATION

239 calories, 23 g fat, 7 g saturated fat, 12 g monounsaturated fat, 2 g polyunsaturated fat, 51 mg cholesterol, 14 g carbohydrate, 3 g NET carbs, 8 g sugar alcohols, 2 g sugar, 3 g fiber, 4 g protein, 156 mg potassium, 93 mg phosphorous, 85 mg sodium, 43 mg magnesium

MACRONUTRIENT RATIO

87% FAT ■ 8% PROTEIN ■ 6% CARBOHYDRATE

Cakes &
Cupcakes

KETO CHOCOLATE CAKE

This recipe makes the perfect rich, moist chocolate layer cake (or cupcakes). Top with Keto Ganache or fluffy Keto Chocolate Buttercream for the perfect ending to a healthy meal.

YIELD: One 9-inch cake or 12 cupcakes (12 servings)

INGREDIENTS

DRY INGREDIENTS

- ½ cup coconut flour (50 g)
- ½ cup cocoa powder (50 g)
- 1½ tsp. cream of tartar
- ½ tsp. baking soda
- ½ tsp. sea salt
- ½ cup erythritol (100 g)
- 2 tsp. grass-fed gelatin

WET INGREDIENTS

- 6 large pastured eggs (room temp)
- 30 drops liquid stevia (to taste)
- ½ cup coconut milk
- ½ cup virgin coconut oil (melted)
- 1 tsp. vanilla extract

DIRECTIONS

1. Preheat oven to 350 F. Grease a 9" cake pan or add liners to a muffin pan.

2. Combine dry ingredients in a medium bowl.

3. In another bowl, combine wet ingredients. Beat on medium speed to combine.

4. Pour dry ingredients into wet and mix on medium until smooth.

5. Pour into prepared pan. Bake 30-35 minutes for cake (22-24 minutes for cupcakes) or until a toothpick comes out clean.

6. Top with **Keto Chocolate Buttercream** *(page 130)*, **Keto Chocolate Ganache** *(page 126)* **or German Chocolate Cake Frosting** *(page 132)*.

NUTRITION INFORMATION

177 calories, 17 g fat, 14 g saturated fat, 2 g monounsaturated fat, 0.5 g polyunsaturated fat, 106 mg cholesterol, 12 g carbohydrate, 2 g NET carbs, 8 g sugar alcohols, 1 g sugar, 2 g fiber, 5 g protein, 176 mg potassium, 93 mg phosphorous, 96 mg sodium, 29 mg magnesium

MACRONUTRIENT RATIO

86% Fat ■ 10% Protein ■ 4% Carbs

KETO YELLOW CAKE

This golden buttery cake the perfect healthy dessert to celebrate a birthday! For a traditional two-layer cake, double the recipe and opt for spring form pans for easy removal.

YIELD: One 8-inch cake or 12 cupcakes (12 servings)

INGREDIENTS

DRY INGREDIENTS

- ½ cup coconut flour (50 g)
- ⅔ cup almond flour (60 g)
- ¼ tsp. sea salt
- ½ tsp. baking soda
- ½ cup erythritol (100 g)

WET INGREDIENTS

- 4 large pastured eggs (room temp).
- ½ tsp. liquid stevia (to taste)
- ¾ cup coconut milk
- 2 tsp. vanilla extract

DIRECTIONS

1. Preheat oven to 350 F. Grease an 8" cake pan or add liners to a muffin pan.

2. In a medium bowl, combine dry ingredients. In another bowl, whisk wet ingredients.

3. Pour dry ingredients into wet. Mix with a handheld mixer on medium until very smooth.

4. Pour batter into prepared pan and bake 30-35 minutes for cake (22-24 minutes for cupcakes) or until a toothpick comes out clean.

5. Top with **Keto Chocolate Buttercream** *(page 130)* **or Cocoa Butter Ganache** *(page 126)*.

NUTRITION INFORMATION

98 calories, 9 g fat, 4 g saturated fat, 2 g monounsaturated fat, 1 g polyunsaturated fat, 70 mg cholesterol, 10 g carbohydrate, 1 g NET carbs, 8 g sugar alcohols, 1 g sugar, 1 g fiber, 3.5 g protein, 73 mg potassium, 61 mg phosphorous, 132 mg sodium, 17 mg magnesium

MACRONUTRIENT RATIO

81% FAT ■ 14% PROTEIN ■ 5% CARBOHYDRATE

KETO MOLTEN CHOCOLATE CAKE

This golden buttery cake the perfect healthy dessert to celebrate a birthday! For a traditional two-layer cake, double the recipe and opt for spring form pans for easy removal.

YIELD: 4 servings

INGREDIENTS

- 3 ounces *Lily's Dark Chocolate Chips*
- ¼ cup grass-fed butter or virgin coconut oil
- 1 large pastured egg + 1 egg yolk
- 3 Tbsp. erythritol, powdered
- 2 Tbsp. grass-fed whey protein powder or bone broth protein powder

DIRECTIONS

1. Preheat oven to 400 F. Bring eggs to room temperature. Grease unbleached parchment paper muffin liners.

2. In a heavy-bottomed saucepan or double boiler, melt the chocolate and butter. Stir until smooth. You may also microwave on high in 20 seconds bursts, until melted.

3. In a medium bowl, whisk the egg, egg yolk, powdered erythritol and protein powder. Beat in chocolate mixture until smooth and glossy.

4. Pour into prepared muffin liners. Bake for 7 minutes (or until puffed up and still a bit moist on top). Do NOT over bake.

5. Let cakes stand for one minute. Invert on to individual serving dishes.

6. Enjoy warm, with fresh raspberries or a scoop of ***Keto Vanilla Bean Ice Cream*** *(page 120).*

NUTRITION INFORMATION

237 calories, 21 g fat, 12 g saturated fat, 4 g monounsaturated fat, 1 g polyunsaturated fat, 140 mg cholesterol, 23 g carbohydrate, 4 g NET carbs, 14 g sugar alcohols, 1 g sugar, 6 g fiber, 8 g protein, 30 mg potassium, 44 mg phosphorous, 109 mg sodium, 2 mg magnesium

MACRONUTRIENT RATIO

81% FAT ■ 13% PROTEIN ■ 6% CARBOHYDRATE

2 NET CARBS | **DAIRY FREE** | **PALEO FRIENDLY**

KETO COCONUT SPONGE CAKE

This coconut lover's dessert has a light, spongy texture — slightly denser than Angel Food Cake. Top with lightly toasted coconut or drizzle with Keto Ganache for a beautiful presentation.

YIELD: One 9-inch cake or Bundt (12 servings)

INGREDIENTS

DRY INGREDIENTS

- ¼ cup coconut flour (30 g)
- ⅔ cup almond flour (60 g)
- ½ cup shredded unsweetened coconut (30 g)
- ⅓ cup vanilla egg white protein powder or grass-fed whey protein powder(30 g)
- ¼ tsp. sea salt
- 1½ tsp. baking powder
- 1 tsp. baking soda
- ¾ cup erythritol (150 g)

WET INGREDIENTS

- 4 egg whites (or ¾ cup liquid egg whites)
- 25 drops liquid stevia
- ½ cup coconut milk
- ½ cup virgin coconut oil (melted)
- ½ tsp. organic coconut extract (optional)

DIRECTIONS

1. Preheat oven to 350 F. Grease a 9" cake or Bundt pan.

2. In a medium bowl, combine dry ingredients (except for the erythritol).

3. In another bowl, add the coconut oil and erythritol. Beat on medium-high to combine. Add the egg whites, stevia and coconut extract. Beat on high for 1 minute.

4. Pour in the dry ingredients and beat to incorporate. Add the coconut milk and beat until smooth.

5. Pour into prepared pan and bake 35-40 minutes or until a toothpick comes out clean.

6. Let cool, then sprinkle with toasted coconut or drizzle with *Keto Chocolate Ganache* *(page 126)*.

NUTRITION INFORMATION

200 calories, 19 g fat, 13 g saturated fat, 3 g monounsaturated fat, 1 g polyunsaturated fat, 0 mg cholesterol, 17 g carbohydrate, 2 g NET carbs, 12 g sugar alcohols, 1 g sugar, 2 g fiber, 6 g protein,177 mg potassium, 88 mg phosphorous, 231 mg sodium, 24 mg magnesium

MACRONUTRIENT RATIO

83% FAT ■ 12% PROTEIN ■ 5% CARBOHYDRATE

KETO TIRAMISU

The classic Italian dessert gets a low-carb makeover with coconut flour lady fingers, covered in a sweet and decadent, full-fat cream filling.

YIELD: One 8" pan (9 servings)

INGREDIENTS

LADY FINGER INGREDIENTS

- 5 large pastured eggs, separated
- ½ cup erythritol, powdered (100 g)
- ½ cup coconut flour, sifted (40 g)
- 1 tsp. vanilla extract

ALMOND-COFFEE REDUCTION

- ¾ cup strong brewed coffee
- 2 tsp. organic almond extract

CRÈME FILLING INGREDIENTS

- 1½ cups organic heavy cream
- 16 oz. organic cream cheese
- 1 tsp. vanilla extract
- 40 drops liquid stevia (to taste)

COCOA FOR DUSTING

- 1 tsp. organic cocoa powder

DIRECTIONS

1. Preheat oven to 375 F. Line a baking sheet with unbleached parchment paper. Grease or line a 9"x9" pan with unbleached parchment. Prepare a pastry bag with a round tip. If you don't have a pastry bag, cut a ¼-inch corner from a large zip-top bag. Bring cream cheese to room temperature.

2. Make the lady fingers. Separate the eggs. Add the whites to a stand mixer or large bowl. Beat until stiff peaks form. In a small bowl, whisk the yolks with the powdered erythritol and vanilla extract. Slowly sift in the coconut flour. Fold the coconut flour mixture into the egg whites to fully incorporate.

3. Scrape batter into pastry bag. Pipe mixture onto prepared baking sheet as 8" long cookies. Transfer to preheated oven. Bake 8-10 minutes or just until golden.

4. Make the coffee-almond extract syrup. Add strong brewed coffee to a small saucepan over medium-high heat. Simmer for 5-8 minutes to reduce. Stir in the almond extract.

5. Make the crème filling. In a small bowl, combine the cream cheese, vanilla and stevia (to taste). Add the heavy cream to a stand mixer or large bowl. Beat on high until stiff peaks form. Fold the cream cheese mixture into the whipped cream.

6. Assemble the tiramisu. Create a layer of lady finger cookies in the bottom of prepared pan. Drizzle with ⅓ of the almond-coffee reduction. Dollop cookies with ⅓ cream cheese mixture and spread to cover. Create two additional layers with remaining cookies, coffee and cream cheese mixture.

7. Cover and refrigerate for at least 8 hours. Dust top of the tiramisu with cocoa powder. Cut into squares and serve.

NUTRITION INFORMATION

374 calories, 37 g fat, 23 g saturated fat, 10 g monounsaturated fat, 2 g polyunsaturated fat, 227 mg cholesterol, 14 g carbohydrate, 3g NET carbs, 11 g sugar alcohols, 1 g sugar, 1g fiber, 8 g protein,160 mg potassium, 138 mg phosphorous, 203 mg sodium, 14 mg magnesium

MACRONUTRIENT RATIO

88% FAT ■ 9% PROTEIN ■ 3% CARBOHYDRATE

KETO CARROT CAKE

If old-fashioned carrot cake takes you back to childhood, you will love this updated version — with less than two grams of sugar per serving!

YIELD: One 8" cake or 12 cupcakes (12 servings)

INGREDIENTS

DRY INGREDIENTS

- 1⅓ cups blanched almond flour (135 g)
- ½ cup erythritol, powdered (85 g)
- 2 tsp. cinnamon
- ½ tsp. baking soda
- ½ tsp. sea salt

WET INGREDIENTS

- 3 large pastured eggs
- 2 Tbsp. virgin coconut oil (melted)
- 2 tsp. vanilla extract
- 40 drops liquid stevia (to taste)
- 1½ cups grated organic carrots (120 g)
- ½ cup pecans, chopped (50 g)

DIRECTIONS

1. Preheat oven 350 F. Grease an 8" round cake pan or prepare a muffin tin with unbleached parchment cupcake liners.

2. In a medium bowl, whisk dry ingredients. In another bowl, add wet ingredients and beat with a hand-held mixer to combine. Add dry ingredients to wet and mix to incorporate. Stir in grated carrots and pecans.

3. Pour batter into prepared pan and bake 30-35 minutes (18-22 minutes for cupcakes) or until a toothpick comes out clean.

4. Let cool and then frost with **Cream Cheese Frosting** *(page 136),* **Fresh Whipped Cream** or **Whipped Coconut Cream** *(page 140)* to achieve the ketogenic Magic Macros.

NUTRITION INFORMATION

186 calories, 16 g fat,4 g saturated fat, 8 g monounsaturated fat, 3 g polyunsaturated fat, 63 mg cholesterol, 16 g carbohydrate, 3 g NET carbs, 10 g sugar alcohols, 2 g sugar, 3.5 g fiber, 6 g protein, 216 mg potassium, 130 mg phosphorous, 217 mg sodium, 55 mg magnesium

MACRONUTRIENT RATIO

80% FAT ■ 13% PROTEIN ■ 7% CARBOHYDRATE

KETO RED VELVET CAKE

This Southern-style favorite gets a healthy makeover with natural red food coloring and keto-friendly sweeteners to create moist, sweet cake with just one gram of sugar.

YIELD: One 9" cake or 12 cupcakes (12 servings)

INGREDIENTS

DRY INGREDIENTS

- 1¼ cup coconut flour, sifted (120 g)
- ¾ cup erythritol, powdered (150 g)
- 2 Tbsp. cocoa powder, sifted (12 g)
- ½ tsp. baking soda
- ½ tsp. baking powder
- ½ tsp. sea salt

WET INGREDIENTS

- 4 large pastured eggs
- 6 Tbsp. grass-fed butter or virgin coconut oil (melted)
- 1 Tbsp. organic red food coloring (like India Tree)
- ½ cup plain coconut yogurt
- 2 tsp. vanilla extract
- 40 drops liquid stevia (to taste)

DIRECTIONS

1. Preheat oven to 350 F. Grease a 9" round cake pan or line a muffin tin with unbleached cupcake liners.

2. In a medium bowl, whisk dry ingredients.

3. In another bowl, add wet ingredients. Beat with a hand-held mixer on medium to fully combine.

4. Add dry ingredients to wet. Blend on medium to incorporate.

5. Pour batter into prepared cake pan or muffin tin. Bake 22-25 minutes for cupcakes (33-35 minutes for cake) or until a toothpick comes out clean.

6. Cool to room temperature and frost with **Keto Cream Cheese Frosting** *(page 136)* or **Coconut Cream Frosting** *(page 140)*.

NUTRITION INFORMATION

144 calories, 14 g fat, 11 g saturated fat, 1 g monounsaturated fat, 0 g polyunsaturated fat, 70 mg cholesterol, 15 g carbohydrate, 2 g NET carbs, 1 g sugar alcohols, 1 g sugar, 2 g fiber, 3 g protein, 95 mg potassium, 66 mg phosphorous, 176 mg sodium, 13 mg magnesium

MACRONUTRIENT RATIO

88% FAT ■ 8% PROTEIN ■ 5% CARBOHYDRATE

KETO POUND CAKE

You won't believe the authentic taste and texture of this dense and buttery pound cake. Perfect on its own or topped with fresh whipped cream. For a tangy twist, stir in poppy seeds and lemon juice.

YIELD: One 9x5" loaf cake (12 servings)

INGREDIENTS

DRY INGREDIENTS

- 1½ cups almond flour (150 g)
- 2 scoops vanilla whey protein powder or bone broth protein powder (40 g)
- ½ cup erythritol, powdered (100 g)
- ¾ tsp. baking powder
- ¼ tsp. sea salt

WET INGREDIENTS

- 3 large pastured eggs
- 6 Tbsp. grass-fed butter or virgin coconut oil (melted)
- ¼ cup. coconut milk
- ½ Tbsp. vanilla extract
- 40 drops liquid stevia (to taste)

DIRECTIONS

1. Preheat oven to 350 F. Grease a 9x5" loaf pan. Line with unbleached parchment paper.

2. In a medium bowl, whisk the almond flour, erythritol, protein powder, baking powder and salt.

3. In another bowl, add the eggs, melted oil or butter, coconut milk, vanilla, and stevia. Beat with a hand-held mixer on medium to fully combine.

4. Add dry ingredients to wet. Blend on medium to incorporate.

5. Pour batter into prepared pan. Bake 40-45 minutes or until a toothpick comes out clean.

6. Cool to room temperature, slice and serve.

NUTRITION INFORMATION

173 calories, 15 g fat, 5 g saturated fat, 6 g monounsaturated fat, 2 g polyunsaturated fat, 71 mg cholesterol, 12 g carbohydrate, 2 g NET carbs, 8 g sugar alcohols, 1 g sugar, 2 g fiber, 7 g protein, 135 mg potassium, 93 mg phosphorous, 166 mg sodium, 39 mg magnesium

MACRONUTRIENT RATIO

78% FAT ■ 17% PROTEIN ■ 5% CARBOHYDRATE

KETO SPICE CAKE

Packed with antioxidant-rich spices, this moist cake is perfect with a cup of hot cocoa or tea. Don't be afraid to add allspice, nutmeg and cardamom for even more flavor and nutritional benefits.

YIELD: One 8" cake or 12 cupcakes (12 servings)

INGREDIENTS

DRY INGREDIENTS

- ½ cup coconut flour (50 g)
- ⅔ cup almond flour (60 g)
- ¼ tsp. sea salt
- ½ tsp. baking soda
- ⅓ cup erythritol (75 g)
- 1 tsp. ground ginger
- 1 tsp. cinnamon
- ½ tsp. cloves

WET INGREDIENTS

- 4 pastured eggs (room temp)
- 1 Tbsp. *Lakanto Maple Flavored Syrup*
- 40 drops liquid stevia (to taste)
- ¾ cup coconut milk
- 2 tsp. vanilla extract

DIRECTIONS

1. Preheat oven to 350 F. Grease an 8" cake pan or 9" Bundt pan or add liners to a muffin pan.

2. In a medium bowl, combine dry ingredients. In another bowl, add wet ingredients. Mix with a hand mixer to combine.

3. Pour dry ingredients into wet and mix with a hand mixer on medium until very smooth.

4. Pour into prepared pan and bake 30-35 minutes for cake (22-24 minutes for cupcakes) or until a toothpick comes out clean.

5. Let cool and then dust with powdered erythritol. Drizzle with **Sugar-Free Lemon Glaze** *(page 142)* or frost with **Keto Vanilla Buttercream** *(page 134)*.

NUTRITION INFORMATION

103 calories, 9 g fat, 5 g saturated fat, 2 g monounsaturated fat, 1 g polyunsaturated fat, 70 mg cholesterol, 9 g carbohydrate, 1 g NET carbs, 6 g sugar alcohols, 0.5 g sugar, 1 g fiber, 4 g protein, 107 mg potassium, 74 mg phosphorous, 184 mg sodium, 24 mg magnesium

MACRONUTRIENT RATIO

82% FAT ■ 15% PROTEIN ■ 4% CARBOHYDRATE

Cookies

KETO ALMOND BUTTER CHOCOLATE CHIP COOKIES

These chocolate chip cookies with chewy centers and crisp edges may become your new favorite! Swap out the almond butter with homemade macadamia butter for a tropical twist on this classic.

YIELD: 12 cookies

INGREDIENTS

- 1 pastured egg + 1 egg yolk
- 1 cup creamy raw almond butter
- ⅔ cup erythritol, powdered (130 g)
- 2 tsp. vanilla extract
- 20 drops liquid stevia (to taste)
- ½ tsp. sea salt
- 1 tsp. baking soda
- ½ tsp. cream of tartar
- 4 Tbsp. *Lily's Dark Chocolate Chips*

DIRECTIONS

1. Preheat oven to 350 F. Line a baking sheet with unbleached parchment paper.

2. In a small bowl, whisk the egg and egg yolk together. In a medium bowl, add the almond butter, erythritol, baking soda, cream of tartar, vanilla, stevia and salt. Pour in the whisked egg. Stir well to combine. Fold in the chocolate chips. Stir to incorporate. Transfer to the refrigerator to chill 10 minutes.

3. Using a tablespoon or cookie scoop, drop 1 Tbsp. balls onto the lined cookie sheet. Leave 2 inches of space between cookies as they will spread.

4. Transfer to oven. Bake 9-11 minutes or until edges begin to brown. Let cookies cool on pan for 5 minutes before serving.

NUTRITION INFORMATION

157 calories, 14 g fat, 2 g saturated fat, 8 g monounsaturated fat, 3 g polyunsaturated fat, 35 mg cholesterol, 17 g carbohydrate, 2 NET carbs, 11 g sugar alcohols, 1 g sugar, 4 g fiber, 6 g protein, 8 mg potassium, 14 mg phosphorous, 165 mg sodium, 11 mg magnesium

MACRONUTRIENT RATIO

80% FAT ■ 14% PROTEIN ■ 6% CARBOHYDRATE

2 NET CARBS | **DAIRY FREE** | **PALEO FRIENDLY**

KETO REAL-DEAL CHOCOLATE CHIP COOKIES

This healthy version of America's best-loved cookie will probably become your go-to favorite! The "secret" ingredient is gelatin, which gives these cookies the "chewiness" we all know and love.

YIELD: 14 cookies

INGREDIENTS

- 1¼ cups blanched almond flour (125 g)
- 1½ Tbsp. coconut flour (10 g)
- 1½ tsp. baking powder
- ¼ tsp. sea salt
- 3 tsp. grass-fed beef gelatin
- ½ cup erythritol, powdered (100 g)
- 6 Tbsp. grass-fed butter or palm shortening
- 1 large pastured egg
- 1 tsp. vanilla extract
- 30 drops liquid stevia
- 2 ounces *Lily's Dark Chocolate Chips*
- ¼ cup pecans, chopped (25 g)

DIRECTIONS

1. Preheat oven to 350 F. Line a baking sheet with unbleached parchment paper. Bring butter to room temperature.

2. In a small bowl, combine the almond flour, coconut flour, baking powder, sea salt and gelatin.

3. In a medium mixing bowl, add the butter and erythritol. Using a hand mixer, cream until combined. Add the egg, vanilla and stevia. Mix again.

4. Pour flour mixture into the creamed butter. Mix to combine. Stir in the chocolate chips and pecans. Transfer to freezer for 10 minutes to chill.

5. Using a tablespoon or a cookie scoop, drop 1 Tbsp. balls onto sheet. Leave 2 inches between cookies. Flatten dough slightly.

6. Transfer to the oven and bake 14-16 minutes to golden. Remove from oven. Cool on a wire rack until firm.

NUTRITION INFORMATION

138 calories, 13 g fat, 4 g saturated fat, 5 g monounsaturated fat, 2 g polyunsaturated fat, 28 mg cholesterol, 16 g carbohydrate, 2 g NET carbs, 11 g sugar alcohols, 1 g sugar, 3 g fiber, 4 g protein, 85 mg potassium, 62 mg phosphorous, 42 mg sodium, 30 mg magnesium

MACRONUTRIENT RATIO

85% FAT ■ 10% PROTEIN ■ 5% CARBOHYDRATE

KETO BROWNIE COOKIES

These uber-chocolaty treats are one part crisp cookie, one part chewy-nutty brownie and 100 percent delicious!

YIELD: 8 cookies

INGREDIENTS

- 2 Tbsp. organic cocoa powder
- ⅛ tsp. baking soda
- ⅛ tsp. sea salt
- ¼ cup erythritol, powdered (50 g)
- 1 large pastured egg
- 8 Tbsp. organic raw creamy almond butter
- 2 Tbsp. grass-fed butter or palm shortening (room temp)
- 15 drops liquid stevia
- ½ tsp. vanilla extract
- ¼ cup raw walnuts, chopped

DIRECTIONS

1. Preheat oven to 350 F. Line a baking sheet with unbleached parchment.

2. In a medium bowl, add the cocoa powder, baking soda, salt and powdered erythritol.

3. Next, add the egg, vanilla, stevia, softened butter and almond butter. Stir well to combine. Add walnuts and stir again.

4. Roll 1 Tbsp. scoops into balls. Place on lined baking sheet about an inch apart. Flatten slightly.

5. Transfer to the oven. Bake for 12-14 minutes or until edges are dry and centers are still slightly moist.

6. Cool on a wire rack. Store in an airtight container in the refrigerator.

NUTRITION INFORMATION

157 calories, 15 g fat, 3 g saturated fat, 7 g monounsaturated fat, 4 g polyunsaturated fat, 34 mg cholesterol, 10 g carbohydrate, 2 g NET carbs, 6 g sugar alcohols, 1 g sugar, 3 g fiber, 5 g protein, 45 mg potassium, 35 mg phosphorous, 87 mg sodium, 21 mg magnesium

MACRONUTRIENT RATIO

83% FAT ■ 13% PROTEIN ■ 4% CARBOHYDRATE

KETO SUNBUTTER COOKIES

With the same taste and texture as the original, this Paleo riff on Peanut Butter cookies has just one net carb and less than a gram of sugar per serving.

YIELD: 12 cookies

INGREDIENTS

- 1 cup *Organic Sunbutter* (unsweetened, unsalted)
- 1 large pastured egg
- ½ cup erythritol, powdered (100 g)
- 30 drops liquid stevia (to taste)
- 1 tsp. vanilla extract
- ¼ tsp. sea salt

DIRECTIONS

1. Preheat oven to 350 F. Line a cookie sheet with unbleached parchment paper.

2. In a medium bowl, add all ingredients. Mix well using a wooden spoon or hand-held mixer.

3. Roll dough into 1-inch balls. Place on lined cookie sheet and depress using a fork. These cookies will not spread much, so you can space them close together.

4. Transfer to oven. Bake 13-15 minutes.

NUTRITION INFORMATION

147 calories, 12 g fat, 1 g saturated fat, 7 g monounsaturated fat, 4 g polyunsaturated fat, 17 mg cholesterol, 11 g carbohydrate, 1 NET carbs, 8 g sugar alcohols, 0 g sugar, 2 g fiber, 5 g protein, 6 mg potassium, 8 mg phosphorous, 26 mg sodium, 11 mg magnesium

MACRONUTRIENT RATIO

92% FAT ■ 3% PROTEIN ■ 5% CARBOHYDRATE

KETO COCONUT MACAROONS

Crispy on the outside with a light-coconut-ty interior, these macaroons are not sticky and cloyingly sweet like traditional macaroons.

YIELD: 18 macaroons

INGREDIENTS

DRY INGREDIENTS

- 1 cup unsweetened shredded coconut (60 g)
- ⅓ cup powdered erythritol (70 g)
- 1 tsp. coconut flour
- ¼ tsp. sea salt

WET INGREDIENTS

- 2 egg whites
- 30 drops liquid stevia
- ½ tsp. vanilla extract

DIRECTIONS

1. Preheat oven to 350 F. Line a cookie sheet with unbleached parchment paper.

2. In a medium bowl, add dry ingredients.

3. In another bowl, add wet ingredients.

4. Add dry ingredients to wet. Stir well to combine. Let mixture stand for 1 minute to set.

5. Scoop out dough by rounded teaspoons. Place on lined cookie sheet. Shape as desired (they will not spread).

6. Transfer to oven. Bake 13-15 minutes or until macaroons begin to brown and are no longer soft in the middle.

7. Allow to cool and then drizzle with melted dark chocolate, if desired.

NUTRITION INFORMATION

44 calories, 4 g fat, 3 g saturated fat, 0 g monounsaturated fat, 0 g polyunsaturated fat, 0 mg cholesterol, 5 g carbohydrate, 0.5 g NET carbs, 4 g sugar alcohols, 0.5 g sugar, 1 g fiber, 1 g protein, 40 mg potassium, 13 mg phosphorous, 38 mg sodium, 6 mg magnesium

MACRONUTRIENT RATIO

87% FAT ■ 8% PROTEIN ■ 5% CARBOHYDRATE

KETO SNICKERDOODLE BITES

This one-bite riff on the classic snickerdoodle is crispy on the outside, pillow-soft on the inside. And don't leave off the coating — it adds a touch of sweetness and the crispy crackles this favorite is known for.

YIELD: 24 one-bite cookies

INGREDIENTS

DRY INGREDIENTS

- 1¼ cups blanched almond flour (120 g)
- 2 tsp. coconut flour (6 g)
- 4 Tbsp. erythritol (50 g)
- 1 tsp. cinnamon
- ¼ tsp. cream of tartar
- ¼ tsp. sea salt
- ¼ tsp. baking soda

WET INGREDIENTS

- 1 large pastured egg
- ¼ cup coconut oil (melted)
- 30 drops liquid stevia
- 1 tsp. vanilla extract

COATING

- ½ Tbsp. cinnamon
- ½ Tbsp. coconut sugar (or erythritol)

DIRECTIONS

1. Preheat oven to 350 F. Line a cookie sheet with unbleached parchment paper.

2. In a medium bowl, combine dry ingredients.

3. In another bowl, add wet ingredients. Mix well with a hand mixer.

4. Add dry ingredients to wet and mix on medium until a dough is formed.

5. In a small bowl, whisk the coating ingredients.

6. Scoop out dough by rounded teaspoons and roll into balls. Roll each ball in cinnamon-sugar mixture. Place coated balls on lined cookie sheet. For the domed effect pictured, do not press dough balls.

7. Transfer to oven. Bake 9-11 minutes for softer cookies or 11-13 minutes for crispy cookies.

NUTRITION INFORMATION

67 calories, 6 g fat, 3 g saturated fat, 2 g monounsaturated fat, 1 g polyunsaturated fat, 9 mg cholesterol, 4 g carbohydrate, 1 g NET carbs, 2 g sugar alcohols, 0.6 g sugar, 1 g fiber, 2 g protein, 58 mg potassium, 38 mg phosphorous, 39 mg sodium, 19 mg magnesium

MACRONUTRIENT RATIO

82% FAT ■ 11% PROTEIN ■ 6% CARBOHYDRATE

KETO GINGER COOKIES

These sweet-n-spicy keto treats combine the crisp bite of ginger snaps with a chewy texture... and all the nostalgia that comes with this internationally-loved cookie.

YIELD: 12 cookies

INGREDIENTS

- 1 large pastured egg + 1 egg yolk
- 1 cup creamy raw almond butter
- 1 tsp. vanilla extract
- 20 drops liquid stevia
- ½ cup erythritol, powdered (100 g)
- ½ tsp. baking soda
- ½ tsp. cream of tartar
- 2 tsp. ginger powder
- ¼ tsp. sea salt

DIRECTIONS

1. Preheat oven to 350 F. Line a baking sheet with unbleached parchment paper.

2. In a medium bowl, whisk together the egg, egg yolk, almond butter, vanilla and stevia.

3. In another bowl, whisk the erythritol, baking soda, cream of tartar, ginger and sea salt.

4. Mix the dry ingredients into the wet until dough is formed. Transfer to the refrigerator. Chill for 10 minutes.

5. Scoop dough by rounded tablespoon onto lined baking sheet. Flatten slightly.

6. Transfer to oven. Bake 9-11 minutes or until edges begin to brown.

7. Cool cookies on pan for 5 minutes before serving.

NUTRITION INFORMATION

138 calories, 12 g fat, 1 g saturated fat, 8 g monounsaturated fat, 3 g polyunsaturated fat, 35 mg cholesterol, 12 g carbohydrate, 2 g NET carbs, 8 g sugar alcohols, 1 g sugar, 3 g fiber, 5 g protein, 22 mg potassium, 13 mg phosphorous, 112 mg sodium, 11 mg magnesium

MACRONUTRIENT RATIO

80% FAT ■ 16% PROTEIN ■ 4% CARBOHYDRATE

KETO FLORENTINE LACE COOKIES

Do you love chewy, bakery-style tea cookies with sweet chocolate drizzle... but you can do without the sugar and grain? This almost sugar-free version gets its chewy goodness from homemade orange marmalade.

YIELD: 12 large (3½") cookies

INGREDIENTS

- 6 Tbsp. organic heavy cream
- 2 Tbsp. grass-fed butter or palm shortening
- ¼ cup erythritol (44 g)
- 1 cup sliced almonds, ground to a sandy texture (80 g)
- 1 Tbsp. almond flour (8 g)
- 2 tsp. coconut flour (6 g)
- ⅛ tsp. sea salt
- 2 Tbsp. **Homemade Sugar-Free Orange Marmalade** *(Page 138)*
- 30 drops liquid stevia
- 1 tsp. vanilla extract
- 2 oz. *Lily's Chocolate Chips*

DIRECTIONS

1. Set rack in the middle of the oven and preheat to 350 F. Line a cookie sheet with unbleached parchment paper.

2. In a medium saucepan, add cream, butter (or shortening) and erythritol. Heat on medium and bring to a boil while whisking. Simmer for 5 minutes until thick and beginning to brown.

3. Add ground almonds, almond flour, coconut flour, sea salt and marmalade. Stir to combine. Stir in vanilla and stevia. Remove from heat. Allow to cool slightly and thicken.

4. Scoop dough by tablespoons and drop onto parchment-lined cookie sheet 3 inches apart. With fingers wet, press cookies into 2-inch circles. The thinner you make them the crispier and chewier they will be.

5. Transfer to oven. Bake until outer edges turn deep brown (about 9 minutes). Watch carefully. They can burn quickly!

6. Remove from oven. Cool on pan for 2 minutes. Transfer cookies on parchment to cooling rack.

7. Melt the chocolate. Microwave for 30-second increments or use a double boiler. Pour melted and slightly cooled chocolate into a zip top bag. Cut a very small hole in the corner of the bag.

8. Drizzle melted chocolate over Florentine cookies. Let cool and harden.

NUTRITION INFORMATION

100 calories, 9 g fat, 4 g saturated fat, 3 g monounsaturated fat, 1 g polyunsaturated fat, 15 mg cholesterol, 9 g carbohydrate, 2 g NET carbs, 5 g sugar alcohols, 0.3 g sugar, 2 g fiber, 2 g protein, 51 mg potassium, 33 mg phosphorous, 41 mg sodium, 17 mg magnesium

MACRONUTRIENT RATIO

86% FAT ■ 7% PROTEIN ■ 7% CARBOHYDRATE

KETO MACADAMIA BISCOTTI

If you enjoy crispy, fragrant biscotti with your coffee, meet your new favorite keto cookie! For the lowest carb count, we used almond extract in place of the classic amaretto.

YIELD: 10 - 12 (5") cookies

INGREDIENTS

DRY INGREDIENTS

- ½ cup powdered erythritol (80 g)
- 2¼ cups blanched almond flour (225 g)
- 2½ ounces macadamia nuts, dry roasted and salted, roughly chopped
- 1 tsp. baking powder
- 1 tsp. grass-fed gelatin

WET INGREDIENTS

- 2 large pastured eggs
- 30 drops liquid stevia
- 4 Tbsp. grass-fed butter or coconut oil (melted)
- 2 tsp. almond extract

CHOCOLATE COATING

- 2 oz. *Lily's Chocolate Chips*

DIRECTIONS

1. Preheat oven to 325 F. Line a cookie sheet with unbleached parchment paper.

2. In a medium bowl, combine dry ingredients. In a small bowl, whisk the melted the butter, eggs, stevia and almond extract.

3. Add wet ingredients to the dry and stir to form dough.

4. Scoop dough onto the prepared cookie sheet. Form dough into an oblong shape, roughly 10x5".

5. Transfer to the oven. Bake for 30 minutes or until firm and golden. Remove and cool completely. Turn oven down to 275 F.

6. Using a sharp knife, slice the biscotti width-wise at about 1-inch intervals to create cookies that are approximately 1x5". If the cookie crumbles, chill in the freezer before cutting.

7. Place biscotti back on baking sheet. Transfer to oven. Bake for 10 minutes. Flip cookies and bake another 10 minutes (or until slices are golden). Let cookies cool until crisp.

8. Melt chocolate in a double boiler. Prepare a baking sheet with parchment.

9. Dip one end of the biscotti into the chocolate to coat. Place on lined cookie sheet to cool.

10. Chill biscotti to ensure coating is fully cooled.

NUTRITION INFORMATION

215 calories, 20 g fat, 5 g saturated fat, 11 g monounsaturated fat, 3 g polyunsaturated fat, 45 mg cholesterol, 13 g carbohydrate, 3 g NET carbs, 6 g sugar alcohols, 1 g sugar, 4 g fiber, 6 g protein, 208 mg potassium, 148 mg phosphorous, 55 mg sodium, 58 mg magnesium

MACRONUTRIENT RATIO

83% FAT ■ 11% PROTEIN ■ 6% CARBOHYDRATE

KETO THIN MINT COOKIES

Love Girl Scout Cookies, but not the trans fat, grains and sugar? You'll swoon over our copycat version with just one gram of sugar per thin and minty cookie!

YIELD: 40 small (2") cookies

INGREDIENTS

DRY INGREDIENTS

- 1 cup almond flour (100 g)
- ¾ cup coconut flour (80 g)
- ½ cup erythritol, powdered (100 g)
- ½ cup organic cocoa powder (50 g)

WET INGREDIENTS

- 1 tsp. organic peppermint extract
- 2 large pastured eggs
- 4 Tbsp. virgin coconut oil (melted)

CHOCOLATE COATING

- 3 oz. *Lily's Chocolate Chips*
- 2 Tbsp. virgin coconut oil
- 2 tsp. organic peppermint extract

DIRECTIONS

1. Preheat oven to 225 F. Line two baking sheets with unbleached parchment paper.

2. In a medium bowl, combine dry ingredients. In another bowl, whisk wet ingredients. Add dry ingredients to the wet. Stir to form dough. Transfer to freezer to chill for 10 minutes.

3. Roll dough between two pieces of parchment paper to a uniform ¼-inch thickness. Remove top parchment.

4. Using a 2-inch diameter cookie cutter, cut out circles and place on prepared baking sheet. Repeat until all dough is used.

5. Bake cookies until firm (about 50-55 minutes). Let cookies continue to crisp in turned-off oven.

6. For the coating, use a double boiler or place a metal bowl over a pot of gently simmering water (bowl should not touch the water). Add remaining coconut oil and chocolate chips. Stir until smooth. Remove from heat and stir in remaining peppermint extract.

7. Use two forks or tongs to dip cookies into chocolate until fully coated. Place dipped cookies on waxed paper. Transfer to freezer. Once set, dip the cookies a second time in the melted chocolate. Return to parchment paper and chill in the freezer again.

8. Store in an airtight container in the refrigerator.

NUTRITION INFORMATION

51 calories, 5 g fat, 3 g saturated fat, 1 g monounsaturated fat, 0.3 g polyunsaturated fat, 11 mg cholesterol, 5 g carbohydrate, 1 g NET carbs, 3 g sugar alcohols, 0.2 g sugar, 1 g fiber, 1 g protein, 46 mg potassium, 24 mg phosphorous, 30 mg sodium, 12 mg magnesium

MACRONUTRIENT RATIO

85% FAT ■ 9% PROTEIN ■ 6% CARBOHYDRATE

KETO BUTTER PECAN COOKIES

Pecan flour is what gives these buttery cookies their rich flavor. You could also use hazelnut flour or macadamia nut flour for two delicious riffs on this classic.

YIELD: 24 (2½") cookies

INGREDIENTS

DRY INGREDIENTS

- 1 cup pecan flour (112 g)
- 1 cup almond flour (112 g)
- ⅔ cup erythritol, powdered (130 g)
- 2 Tbsp. coconut sugar, powdered (24 g)
- 4 tsp. coconut flour (16 g)
- ½ tsp. baking soda
- ¼ tsp. sea salt

WET INGREDIENTS

- 1 large pastured egg
- 12 Tbsp. grass-fed butter or palm shortening(melted)
- 1 Tbsp. vanilla extract
- 30 drops liquid stevia (to taste)

MIX IN

- ½ cup pecans, chopped (50 g)

DIRECTIONS

1. Preheat oven to 350 F. Line a cookie sheet with unbleached parchment paper. Set oven rack in middle.

2. In a medium bowl, whisk dry ingredients. In another bowl, whisk wet ingredients.

3. Stir dry ingredients into wet. Fold in chopped pecans. Chill the dough to facilitate shaping (if not chilled, the cookies will spread more).

4. Scoop soft dough by tablespoons and drop onto parchment-lined cookie sheet 3" apart.

5. Transfer to oven. Bake 9-11 minutes (until outer edges turn golden brown). Remove from oven. Cool on pan for 2 minutes, then transfer to a wire rack.

NUTRITION INFORMATION

105 calories, 11 g fat, 4 g saturated fat, 4 g monounsaturated fat, 2 g polyunsaturated fat, 24 mg cholesterol, 8 g carbohydrate, 1 g NET carbs, 6 g sugar alcohols, 1 g sugar, 1 g fiber, 1 g protein, 33 mg potassium, 23 mg phosphorous, 98 mg sodium,8 mg magnesium

MACRONUTRIENT RATIO

91% FAT ■ 4% PROTEIN ■ 6% CARBOHYDRATE

Brownies & Bars

KETO LEMON CHEESECAKE BARS

This traditional-style cheesecake is made with real cream cheese. You co
make it dairy-free by using the filling in our "Cheese-Less" Cheesecake
recipes (although divide the recipe in half for the right proportion).

YIELD: One 8x8" pan (16 servings)

INGREDIENTS

SHORTBREAD CRUST

- 1½ cups almond flour (150 g)
- ¼ cup grass-fed butter or palm shortening, chilled
- ¼ cup erythritol (45 g)
- 10 drops liquid stevia
- ¼ tsp. sea salt
- ½ tsp. organic psyllium husk powder or xanthan gum (optional, reduces breakage)

FILLING

- 12 ounces organic cream cheese
- ¼ cup erythritol, powdered (50 g)
- 1 large pastured egg
- 2 Tbsp. lemon juice + 1 tsp. zest
- 2 Tbsp. organic cream or coconut milk (full fat)
- ¼ tsp. lemon extract
- 30 drops liquid stevia

DIRECTIONS

1. Preheat oven to 350 F. Line the bottom of an 8x8" pan with unbleached parchment paper. Bring cream cheese to room temperature.

2. In a food processor, add the crust ingredients and pulse until dough is formed.

3. Press dough evenly into the bottom of the parchment-lined pan. Transfer to oven to par-bake for 10 minutes. Remove from oven to cool. Reduce oven to 275 F.

4. Make the filling. Add the cream cheese to a medium bowl and beat with an electric mixer until smooth. Add remaining filling ingredients. Beat until silky smooth.

5. Spread filling over cooled crust. Bake 25-30 minutes – the filling should just begin to set.

6. Cool on the counter for 30 minutes. Then chill for 2 hours. Using a spatula, lift the chilled bar out of the pan. Cut into squares using a sharp, non-serrated knife.

NUTRITION INFORMATION

161 calories, 16 g fat, 7 g saturated fat, 6 g monounsaturated fat, 2 g polyunsaturated fat, 47 mg cholesterol, 9 g carbohydrate, 1.5 NET carbs, 6 g sugar alcohols, 0.4 g sugar, 1 g fiber, 4 g protein, 93 mg potassium, 72 mg phosphorous, 120 mg sodium, 25 mg magnesium

MACRONUTRIENT RATIO

86% FAT ■ 10% PROTEIN ■ 4% CARBOHYDRATE

KETO COOKIE DOUGH BLONDIES

These fat-rich blondies are like biting into the cookie dough chunks in a carton of ice cream. For best results, chill after baking and cut into squares. Serve chilled.

YIELD: One 8x8" in pan (16 servings)

INGREDIENTS

DRY INGREDIENTS

- ½ cup almond flour, sifted (50 g)
- ¼ cup coconut flour (20 g)
- ½ cup erythritol, powdered (100 g)
- ½ tsp. baking soda
- ¼ tsp. sea salt

WET INGREDIENTS

- 2 large pastured eggs
- 1 package (7 oz) **Let's Do Organic Creamed Coconut**
- 2 Tbsp. coconut oil or grass-fed butter (melted)
- 2 oz. cocoa butter (melted)
- 2 tsp. vanilla extract
- 30 drops liquid stevia (to taste)

Ingredients continued...

TOPPING & FOLD-IN INGREDIENTS

- 1 Tbsp. unsweetened shredded coconut (4 g)
- ½ cup *Lily's Dark Chocolate Chips*

DIRECTIONS

1. Preheat oven to 350 F. Line the bottom of an 8x8" pan with unbleached parchment paper. Place creamed coconut packet in a bowl of warm water to soften.

2. In a medium bowl, whisk dry ingredients. In another bowl, combine wet ingredients. Beat on medium speed to fully incorporate.

3. Add dry ingredients to wet and beat on medium speed to combine. Fold in chocolate chips (reserve some for topping).

4. Spread the batter into prepared pan. Top with remaining chocolate chunks and coconut.

5. Transfer to oven and bake 22-25 minutes or until a toothpick inserted in the center comes out clean. Cool completely before serving. Best served chilled.

NUTRITION INFORMATION

263 calories, 25 g fat, 19 g saturated fat, 3 g monounsaturated fat, 1 g polyunsaturated fat, 26 mg cholesterol, 15 g carbohydrate, 3 NET carbs, 7 g sugar alcohols, 2 g sugar, 6 g fiber, 2 g protein, 40 mg potassium, 31 mg phosphorous, 94 mg sodium, 11 mg magnesium

MACRONUTRIENT RATIO

92% FAT ■ 3% PROTEIN ■ 5% CARBOHYDRATE

KETO MAGIC COOKIE BARS

With seven layers of caramel-coconut-chocolate goodness, this version of the old-fashioned classic cookie bar has all the crave-able flavors... minus the carbs and sugar.

YIELD: One 8x8" pan (9 servings)

INGREDIENTS

CARAMEL INGREDIENTS

- 2 Tbsp. grass-fed butter
- ¼ cup erythritol (50 g)
- 1 Tbsp. organic heavy cream
- 1 tsp. xanthan gum (optional)

GANACHE INGREDIENTS

- 3 ounces *Lily's Chocolate Chips*
- 1 Tbsp. organic heavy cream

CRUST INGREDIENTS

- ⅓ cup coconut flour (40 g)
- ½ cup blanched almond flour (50 g)
- 2 Tbsp. grass-fed butter
- 1 large pastured egg
- 1 Tbsp. erythritol (12 g)

Ingredients continued...

COCONUT CRÈME INGREDIENTS

- 2 Tbsp. coconut butter
- 6 Tbsp. coconut milk
- 2 Tbsp. erythritol
- 15 drops liquid stevia

TOPPINGS

- ¼ cup unsweetened shredded coconut
- ½ cup pecans, chopped
- 3 Tbsp. *Lily's Chocolate Chips*

DIRECTIONS

1. Preheat oven to 350 F. Line an 8x8" pan with unbleached parchment paper.

2. Make the caramel. In a small saucepan over low heat, add the butter, erythritol, cream and xanthan gum (if using). Simmer for 2 minutes until golden. Remove from heat.

3. Make the crust. Add the coconut flour, almond flour, egg, butter and erythritol to a small bowl. Stir to form dough. Press dough into bottom of the prepared pan. Transfer to the oven. Bake 10 minutes. Cool on a wire rack.

4. Make the ganache. Melt the chocolate chips with 1 Tbsp. cream using a double boiler (or 15-20 second bursts in the microwave).

5. Make the coconut crème. Whisk 6 Tbsp. cream, coconut butter and stevia to form a smooth mixture.

6. Spread ganache over the pre-baked crust. Top with chopped pecans. Drizzle with caramel sauce. Pour coconut crème over. Sprinkle with shredded coconut. Top with chocolate chips.

7. Transfer to oven and bake 20 minutes. Cool on a wire rack for 30 minutes. Refrigerate for 1 hour before cutting into squares.

NUTRITION INFORMATION

271 calories, 27 g fat, 14 g saturated fat, 8 g monounsaturated fat, 2 g polyunsaturated fat, 58 mg cholesterol, 16 g carbohydrate, 3 NET carbs, 8 g sugar alcohols, 1 g sugar, 5 g fiber, 4 g protein, 1120 mg potassium, 79 mg phosphorous, 61 mg sodium, 31 mg magnesium

MACRONUTRIENT RATIO

90% FAT ■ 6% PROTEIN ■ 4% CARBOHYDRATE

KETO REAL-DEAL BROWNIES

You won't believe these rich, chocolate brownies are keto. With their dense-fudgy centers and shiny crackled tops, they taste just like the original!

YIELD: One 8x8" pan (9 servings)

INGREDIENTS

DRY INGREDIENTS

- ½ cup blanched almond flour (50 g)
- ½ cup erythritol, powdered (100 g)
- ½ tsp. non-aluminum baking powder
- ¼ tsp. sea salt

WET INGREDIENTS

- 5 oz. **Lily's Dark Chocolate Chips**
- 8 Tbsp. grass-fed butter or coconut oil (75 g)
- 1 tsp. vanilla extract
- 2 large pastured eggs + 1 egg yolk
- 30 drops liquid stevia (to taste)

DIRECTIONS

1. Preheat oven to 350 F. Grease an 8 x 8 inch pan and line with unbleached parchment paper. Make an ice bath by filling a 9 x9 or larger pan with ice water. Powder the erythritol.

2. Melt the chocolate with the butter over a double boiler or in a glass bowl in the microwave in 20 seconds bursts.

3. In a medium bowl, whisk together the erythritol, baking powder, sea salt and almond flour.

4. Pour in the melted chocolate-butter mixture, vanilla and stevia (to taste), whisking well.

5. Add the eggs and egg yolk, one at a time, whisking thoroughly after each until batter is thick and glossy.

6. Scrape into prepared pan and bake 17-20 minutes.

7. Transfer to ice bath for 20 minutes to set.

8. Slice and serve.

NUTRITION INFORMATION

210 calories, 20 g fat, 10 g saturated fat, 5 g monounsaturated fat, 1 g polyunsaturated fat, 97 mg cholesterol, 22 g carbohydrate, 3 NET carbs, 14 g sugar alcohols, 0 g sugar, 5 g fiber, 4 g protein, 93 mg potassium, 80 mg phosphorous, 153 mg sodium, 18 mg magnesium

MACRONUTRIENT RATIO

86% FAT ■ 8% PROTEIN ■ 6% CARBOHYDRATE

KETO ALMOND BUTTER BROWNIES

These ooey-gooey brownies are egg free, grain free, dairy free and very low in sugar — less than one gram per serving!

YIELD: One 8x8" pan (9 servings)

INGREDIENTS

DRY INGREDIENTS

- 3 Tbsp. coconut flour, sifted (18 g)
- ½ cup erythritol, powdered (100 g)
- ¼ cup cocoa powder (28 g)
- ½ tsp. baking powder
- ½ tsp. baking soda
- ¼ tsp. sea salt

WET INGREDIENTS

- 10 Tbsp. water
- 1 tsp. grass-fed gelatin
- 1 cup creamy raw almond butter
- 1 tsp. liquid stevia (to taste)
- 1 tsp. vanilla extract
- 2 Tbsp. *Lily's Dark Chocolate Chips* (melted)

Ingredients continued...

TOPPINGS (OPTIONAL)

- 2 Tbsp. *Lily's Dark Chocolate Chips*
- 1 oz. lightly toasted walnuts or pecans, chopped
- *Low Carb Caramel* (page 128)

DIRECTIONS

1. Preheat oven to 325 F. Line the bottom of an 8x8" pan with unbleached parchment paper.

2. In a medium bowl, combine dry ingredients. In another bowl, add the water and sprinkle in the gelatin. Let stand 5 minutes. Add almond butter, vanilla, stevia and melted chocolate. Mix well using a hand-held mixer.

3. Pour the dry ingredients into the wet and mix well to combine.

4. Spread brownie batter into prepared pan. Top with chocolate chips and nuts, optional.

5. Transfer to oven. Bake 30-35 minutes or until edges pull away and center is set. If you prefer brownies fudgy and moist inside, remove when center is not quite set (about 30 minutes). Place on a wire rack to cool

6. Drizzle with *Low Carb Caramel* (page128) and top with chopped pecans, if desired. Serve.

NUTRITION INFORMATION

202 calories, 17 g fat, 3 g saturated fat, 10 g monounsaturated fat, 4 g polyunsaturated fat, 0 mg cholesterol, 17 g carbohydrate, 3 NET carbs, 9 g sugar alcohols, 2 g sugar, 6 g fiber, 7 g protein, 76 mg potassium, 40 mg phosphorous, 136 mg sodium, 28 mg magnesium

MACRONUTRIENT RATIO

80% FAT ■ 14% PROTEIN ■ 6% CARBOHYDRATE

Pies & Tarts

KETO SUPERFOOD BERRY CHOCOLATE TARTS

Rich chocolate crème filling over a flaky chocolate crust and topped with a sweet berry sauce... these shareable tarts make a beautiful presentation, perfect for holidays and special occasions.

YIELD: Eight 4¾" tarts (32 servings)

INGREDIENTS

CHOCOLATE CRUST

- 3 cups blanched almond flour (300 g)
- ½ cup coconut oil (melted)
- ¼ cup erythritol, powdered (50 g)
- 1 Tbsp. vanilla extract
- 6 Tbsp. organic cocoa powder (36 g)
- 20 drops liquid stevia
- ½ tsp. sea salt
- 1 tsp. grain-free baking powder
- 2 Tbsp. coconut milk

FILLING

- 1 package **Let's Do Organic Creamed Coconut** (200 g) or coconut butter, softened
- 1 carton (8½ oz.) **Aroy-D Coconut Milk**
- 2 oz. cocoa butter or coconut oil (melted)
- 2 Tbsp. lemon juice
- 1 Tbsp. vanilla extract
- 4 Tbsp. cocoa powder (24 g)
- ¼ cup erythritol, powdered (50 g)
- 30 drops liquid stevia

Ingredients continued...

SAUCE

- 1 cup frozen organic raspberries
- 1 Tbsp. lemon juice
- 1 Tbsp. coconut oil
- 1 tsp. vanilla extract
- 15 drops liquid stevia

GARNISH (OPTIONAL)

- Mint leaves
- A few fresh blackberries

DIRECTIONS

1. Preheat oven to 350 F. Grease 8 fluted mini tart pans (pans should be 4 to 5 inches).

2. In a food processor, add the crust ingredients. Pulse until the dough comes together.

3. Divide dough among tart pans. Press into the bottom of each tart pan. Ensure dough gets into the fluted sides. Transfer to oven and bake for 10 minutes. Set aside to cool.

4. Prepare the filling. Add all of the filling ingredients to a food processor or blender (preferred). Process until very smooth.

5. Scoop out the filling with a ladle and spread onto each tart. Leave ¼-inch of the crust still showing. Transfer to the refrigerator. Chill for 4 hours.

6. Make the berry sauce. Add sauce ingredients to a small saucepan over medium-low heat for 10 minutes. Remove from heat and let cool. Pulse in blender or food processor to purée.

7. Spread cooled sauce onto tarts, and garnish with a berry or mint leaf, if desired. Cut each tart into 4 servings.

NUTRITION INFORMATION

216 calories, 21 g fat, 13 g saturated fat, 4 g monounsaturated fat, 1 g polyunsaturated fat, 0 mg cholesterol, 10 g carbohydrate, 3 NET carbs, 3 g sugar alcohols, 2 g sugar, 4 g fiber, 3 g protein, 122 mg potassium, 74 mg phosphorous, 41 mg sodium, 37 mg magnesium

MACRONUTRIENT RATIO

89% FAT ■ 5% PROTEIN ■ 6% CARBOHYDRATE

KETO LEMON TARTS

Sweet lemon curd sits atop a quick-baked macadamia-shortbread crust for a bright and refreshing elegant summer dessert. For a twist, try with key limes or Meyer lemons.

YIELD: Three 4-5" tarts or One 9" tart (6 servings)

INGREDIENTS

FILLING

- ¼ cup erythritol (42 g)
- 30 drops liquid stevia
- 2 large pastured eggs
- 2 large egg yolks
- 6 Tbsp. grass-fed butter or palm shortening
- ½ cup lemon juice

CRUST

- ¾ cup shredded unsweetened coconut (45 g)
- 4½ ounces roasted macadamia nuts
- 1 large pastured egg
- 1 Tbsp. erythritol (12 g)

DIRECTIONS

1. Preheat oven to 400 F. Prepare three 4-5" tart pans or one 9" tart pan by greasing.

2. Make the crust. Add all crust ingredients to a food processor. Process until a sticky dough is formed.

3. Press the dough into the tart pan or pans. Transfer to the oven. Bake 5-7 minutes, just until golden.

4. Make the lemon curd. Add the remaining erythritol, lemon juice, eggs and egg yolks to a medium saucepan. Whisk to combine. Add the butter. Turn heat to low and whisk to melt the butter. Do not turn heat too high or forget to whisk, or your eggs will scramble!

5. When the butter has melted, turn the heat to medium high. Whisk continuously until mixture thickens. Remove from heat.

6. Pour lemon curd into tart pan or pans, smoothing the top. Transfer to the refrigerator. Chill for at least one hour.

7. Garnish with mint or a few fresh berries and serve.

NUTRITION INFORMATION

401 calories, 40 g fat, 19 g saturated fat, 17 g monounsaturated fat, 1 g polyunsaturated fat, 0 mg cholesterol, 16 g carbohydrate, 4 g NET carbs, 8 g sugar alcohols, 3 g sugar, 4 g fiber, 7 g protein, 220 mg potassium, 144 mg phosphorous, 179 mg sodium, 43 mg magnesium

MACRONUTRIENT RATIO

89% FAT ■ 7% PROTEIN ■ 4% CARBOHYDRATE

KETO KEY LIME PIE

As a Florida native, this dessert has a special place in my heart. With its puckery filling and shortbread crust, this sweet and creamy tropical treat is the perfect summer dessert.

YIELD: One 8" pie (12 servings)

INGREDIENTS

SWEETENED CONDENSED MILK

- 6 Tbsp. grass-fed butter (melted)
- ⅓ cup erythritol (70 g)
- 1 cup organic heavy cream
- 30 drops liquid stevia

CRUST

- 1½ cups blanched almond flour (150 g)
- 1 Tbsp. erythritol
- ¼ cup grass-fed butter (melted)

KEY LIME FILLING

- 4 large pastured eggs
- ½ cup organic heavy cream
- ½ cup Key lime juice (fresh or bottled)

DIRECTIONS

1. Preheat oven to 325 F. Prepare an 8" spring-form pan by greasing and placing unbleached parchment in the bottom.

2. Make the sweetened condensed milk. In a small saucepan over medium heat, add the butter, erythritol and cream. Bring to a boil. Turn heat down and simmer for 20 minutes, whisking occasionally. Add the stevia.

3. Make the crust. Add the crust ingredients to a medium mixing bowl. Stir to combine and form a dough.

4. Press dough into the bottom of prepared pan. Push dough up the outer rim roughly ¾ inch to form the sides of the crust. Poke a few holes in the bottom of the crust. Transfer to preheated oven. Bake for 12 minutes or just until golden. (Do not overbake!)

5. Return to the saucepan. The mixture should be reduced by ⅓. Transfer to a container and chill to room temperature.

6. Remove par-baked crust from oven. Turn oven down to 300 F.

7. Make the key lime filling. In a medium bowl, add the eggs and sweetened condensed milk. Using a hand mixer, blend on medium to combine. With the mixer on low, drizzle in the remaining ½ cup cream and the key lime juice. Add additional stevia (to taste).

8. Scrape filling into par-baked crust. Bake 28-32 minutes or until barely set. Transfer Key Lime Pie to the counter. Cool for 20 minutes, then refrigerate for at least 2 hours.

9. Serve with fresh whipped cream, if desired.

NUTRITION INFORMATION

293 calories, 29 g fat, 14 g saturated fat, 11 g monounsaturated fat, 3 g polyunsaturated fat, 137 mg cholesterol, 11 g carbohydrate, 3 g NET carbs, 6 g sugar alcohols, 1 g sugar, 2 g fiber, 6 g protein, 158 mg potassium, 122 mg phosphorous, 102 mg sodium, 43 mg magnesium

MACRONUTRIENT RATIO

88% FAT ■ 8% PROTEIN ■ 4% CARBOHYDRATE

KETO CHOCOLATE SILK PIE

With its rich chocolate crust and creamy mousse filling, this pie is a chocolate-lover's dream. And it is a cinch to make!

YIELD: One 9" pie (12 servings)

INGREDIENTS

FILLING

- 4 oz. organic baker's chocolate
- ¾ cup grass-fed salted butter (room temp)
- ¼ cup erythritol, powdered (50 g)
- 30 drops liquid stevia
- 3 large pastured eggs

CRUST

- 1½ cups blanched almond flour (150 g)
- ¼ cup organic cocoa powder (24 g)
- 1 Tbsp. erythritol
- ¼ cup grass-fed butter (melted)
- 1 large pastured egg
- 20 drops liquid stevia

DIRECTIONS

1. Preheat oven to 350 F. Grease a 9" spring-form pan.

2. Over a double boiler, melt the chocolate. In a separate pot, melt ¼ cup of the butter for the crust.

3. Make the crust. In a small bowl, add the crust ingredients. Mix well until a dough is formed.

4. Press dough into greased pan. Push dough about ½" up the sides of the pan. Poke holes in the bottom of the crust. Transfer to oven. Bake 8-10 minutes. Cool completely.

5. In a large bowl or stand mixer, add the powdered erythritol and softened butter. Mix on medium-high for 1 minute, scraping down the sides, until pale yellow and fluffy.

6. Bring melted chocolate to room temperature. Very important – if you add the chocolate when warm, it will melt the butter and you will have a soupy pie!

7. Pour cooled liquid chocolate, remaining stevia and vanilla extract into the creamed butter mixture. Add a little at a time, while beating at medium-high speed.

8. Add the eggs, one at a time, mixing on high speed. The mixture should be light and fluffy. Adjust sweetness to taste.

9. Scrape chocolate filling mixture into cooled crust. Chill 2 hours. Serve with fresh whipped cream and stevia-sweetened chocolate chips, if desired.

   NOTE: This recipe contains raw eggs. Consuming raw eggs may increase your risk for foodborne illness.

NUTRITION INFORMATION

283 calories, 28 g fat, 13 g saturated fat, 10 g monounsaturated fat, 3 g polyunsaturated fat, 108 mg cholesterol, 16 g carbohydrate, 3 g NET carbs, 9 g sugar alcohols, 1 g sugar, 4 g fiber, 7 g protein, 231 mg potassium, 154 mg phosphorous, 127 mg sodium, 79 mg magnesium

MACRONUTRIENT RATIO

86% FAT ■ 9% PROTEIN ■ 4% CARBOHYDRATE

Soufflé, Mousse & Custard

KETO CHOCOLATE SOUFFLÉS

These light and chocolaty soufflés make the perfect not-too-filling dessert. Get them to the table quick — they do tend to fall!

YIELD: Four 4-ounce soufflés (4 servings)

INGREDIENTS

- 1 Tbsp. organic cocoa powder
- 2½ ounces *Lily's Dark Chocolate Chips*
- 3 Tbsp. virgin coconut oil
- 1 tsp. vanilla extract
- 1 Tbsp. coconut milk
- 2 large pastured eggs, separated
- ⅛ tsp. cream of tartar
- 1 pinch sea salt

DIRECTIONS

1. Preheat oven to 375 degrees F. Lightly grease a 4-ounce ramekin for each soufflé serving. Dust with cocoa powder (this will help the soufflé climb the sides).

2. In a double boiler or a bowl set over a pan of simmering water, add the chocolate chips and coconut oil. Stir until smooth.

3. Remove from heat. Stir in coconut milk and vanilla. Whisk egg yolks into melted chocolate mixture one at a time.

4. In a medium mixing bowl, add the egg whites, cream of tartar and salt. Beat with a hand mixer on medium until stiff peaks form (about 3 minutes).

5. Gently fold the whipped whites into the melted chocolate mixture. Spoon into ramekins. Transfer to oven.

6. Bake 15-17 minutes until set. Serve immediately.

NUTRITION INFORMATION

208 calories, 20 g fat, 14 g saturated fat, 2 g monounsaturated fat, 1 g polyunsaturated fat, 106 mg cholesterol, 12 g carbohydrate, 3 g NET carbs, 4 g sugar alcohols, 0.3 g sugar, 5 g fiber, 5 g protein, 73 mg potassium, 61 mg phosphorous, 55 mg sodium, 11 mg magnesium

MACRONUTRIENT RATIO

85% FAT ■ 9% PROTEIN ■ 6% CARBOHYDRATE

KETO CHOCOLATE MOUSSE

*This could arguably be the richest, silkiest chocolate mousse ever created!
Be sure to add the gelatin very slowly to avoid clumping.*

YIELD: Four 4-ounce servings

INGREDIENTS

- 1¼ cups organic heavy cream
- 3 oz. *Lily's Chocolate Chips*
- 1 Tbsp. organic cocoa powder
- 1 Tbsp. grass-fed gelatin
- ½ tsp. vanilla extract

DIRECTIONS

1. In a medium saucepan, heat the cream over medium-low heat. Upon simmering, add the chocolate chips and cocoa powder.

2. Remove from heat. Stir with a silicone spatula until chocolate is fully melted and incorporated.

3. Slowly whisk in gelatin, a little at a time, to prevent clumping. Stir in vanilla. Pour into four, 4-ounce serving dishes. Transfer to the refrigerator to chill for 2-3 hours.

4. Serve with fresh whipped cream, a mint sprig or a couple berries.

NUTRITION INFORMATION

349 calories, 34 g fat, 21 g saturated fat, 8 g monounsaturated fat, 1 g polyunsaturated fat, 102 mg cholesterol, 16 g carbohydrate, 5 g NET carbs, 5 g sugar alcohols, 0.2 g sugar, 6 g fiber, 5 g protein, 76 mg potassium, 56 mg phosphorous, 32 mg sodium, 12 mg magnesium

MACRONUTRIENT RATIO

88% FAT ■ 5% PROTEIN ■ 6% CARBOHYDRATE

KETO CRÈME BRÛLEÉ

You won't believe how close to the original our version of this all-time classic dessert tastes. Snap into the crispy, carmelized topping, scoop out a spoonful of sweet and creamy custard and enjoy the bliss.

YIELD: Six 4-ounce brûlée (6 servings)

INGREDIENTS

CRÈME FILLING

- ½ cup erythritol (98 g)
- 20 drops liquid stevia
- 1 tsp vanilla extract
- 1 vanilla bean, scraped
- 2 cups organic heavy cream
- 6 large pastured egg yolks

CARAMEL BRÛLÉE TOPPING

- 1 Tbsp. erythritol (12 g)
- ½ Tbsp. coconut sugar

DIRECTIONS

1. Preheat oven to 325 degrees F. Prepare a 4-ounce ramekin for each serving of crème brûlée. Place the ramekins in a large cake pan or roasting pan. Reserve 1 Tbsp. erythritol for topping.

2. In a medium saucepan, combine heavy cream, vanilla and vanilla bean, and half of the erythritol. Bring to a boil, while whisking continuously. Remove from heat. Allow to cool slightly.

3. Combine the egg yolks and remaining erythritol in a small bowl. With a ladle, slowly dribble the hot cream in a steady stream into the eggs, while quickly whisking the two together. This gradually raises the temperature of the egg and slightly cools the cream, without cooking the eggs.

4. Return mixture to saucepan over low heat and cook until thick enough to coat the back of a spoon.

5. Fill ramekins ⅞ full. Pour water into the pan so that it comes halfway up the ramekins. Transfer to oven. Bake until barely set (approximately 35 minutes).

6. Remove from oven. Combine remaining erythritol with coconut sugar. Sprinkle mixture over the tops.

7. Return to oven and broil for 1-2 minutes to create a crisp shell. You may also caramelize with a kitchen torch. Serve.

NUTRITION INFORMATION

333 calories, 34 g fat, 20 g saturated fat, 10 g monounsaturated fat, 2 g polyunsaturated fat, 318 mg cholesterol, 18 g carbohydrate, 4 g NET carbs, 14 g sugar alcohols, 1 g sugar, 0 g fiber, 4 g protein, 80 mg potassium, 116 mg phosphorous, 40 mg sodium, 6 mg magnesium

MACRONUTRIENT RATIO

90% FAT ■ 5% PROTEIN ■ 5% CARBOHYDRATE

Candies

KETO ALMOND JOY BARS

The addictively-delicious trifecta of coconut, almond and dark chocolate... now keto-friendly and made with health-promoting ingredients.

YIELD: 24 bars

INGREDIENTS

FILLING

- 1 cup coconut milk
- 60 drops liquid stevia
- 2 tsp. vanilla extract
- 2½ cups unsweetened shredded coconut (150 g)
- 50 raw almonds

CHOCOLATE COATING

- 8 ounces *Lily's Chocolate Chips*
- 2 ounces cocoa butter

DIRECTIONS

1. Line a baking sheet with unbleached parchment paper or prepare a candy bar mold.

2. In a medium bowl, mix coconut milk, liquid stevia and 1 tsp vanilla extract. Stir in shredded coconut.

3. Scoop 1-tablespoon portions of coconut mixture and form into a log. Set on parchment and repeat. Otherwise, spoon mixture into a candy bar mold.

4. Top each with 2 almonds. Place in the freezer to set for about 10 minutes.

5. Bring an inch of water to a boil in a small sauce pan. Top with a double boiler or stainless steel bowl that does not touch the water. Add cocoa butter and chocolate chips. Stir well until melted. Add remaining vanilla. Adjust sweetness to taste. Stir well and set aside.

6. Remove coconut-almond bars from freezer. Carefully place one bar on a fork and dip into melted chocolate. Use a spoon to coat all sides, if necessary. Allow excess to drip off and return bar to the parchment sheet.

7. Once all logs are coated, return to the refrigerator. Chill for 1 hour.

NUTRITION INFORMATION

338 calories, 33 g fat, 23 g saturated fat, 2 g monounsaturated fat, 1 g polyunsaturated fat, 0 mg cholesterol, 19 g carbohydrate, 5 g NET carbs, 4 g sugar alcohols, 2 g sugar, 9 g fiber, 4 g protein, 189 mg potassium, 84 mg phosphorous, 10 mg sodium, 40 mg magnesium

MACRONUTRIENT RATIO

89% FAT ■ 5% PROTEIN ■ 6% CARBOHYDRATE

KETO TURTLES

Crunchy pecans, sweet chocolate and gooey caramel create the crave-worthy, candy-shop treat... now made ketogenic.

YIELD: 8 turtles

INGREDIENTS

- 1½ oz. raw pecans
- 1 Tbsp. organic heavy cream
- 3 Tbsp. erythritol, powdered
- 3 Tbsp. grass-fed butter
- ½ Tbsp. coconut palm sugar
- ½ tsp. xanthan gum
- 2 oz. **Lily's Chocolate Chips**

DIRECTIONS

1. Line a baking sheet with unbleached parchment paper. Arrange pecans in clusters of 3 on the parchment and set aside. Powder the erythritol.

2. Make the caramel. Melt butter in a small saucepan on medium-high heat. Add the erythritol, cream, coconut sugar and xanthan gum. Whisk the mixture until the caramel begins to bubble and darken (about 2 minutes). Set aside to cool.

3. Add 1 inch of water to a double boiler or small saucepan with a stainless steel bowl on top. Bring to a boil.

4. As the water comes to a boil, drizzle about 2 teaspoons of caramel over each pecan cluster. Place in the refrigerator to set.

5. Add chocolate chips to the double boiler. Stir until melted.

6. Spoon melted chocolate over caramel-covered pecans. Return to the refrigerator to set.

NUTRITION INFORMATION

111 calories, 11 g fat, 5 g saturated fat, 3 g monounsaturated fat, 1 g polyunsaturated fat, 14 mg cholesterol, 11 g carbohydrate, 2 g NET carbs, 6 g sugar alcohols, 1 g sugar, 3 g fiber, 1 g protein, 25 mg potassium, 17 mg phosphorous, 32 mg sodium, 7 mg magnesium

MACRONUTRIENT RATIO

89% FAT ▪ 4% PROTEIN ▪ 7% CARBOHYDRATE

KETO ALMOND BUTTER FUDGE

Decadent and sweet, this quick and easy nut butter fudge comes together in minutes.

YIELD: One 9x5" pan (12 servings)

INGREDIENTS

NUT BUTTER FUDGE

- 1 cup smooth almond butter
- 1 cup virgin coconut oil
- ¼ cup unsweetened vanilla almond milk
- ⅛ tsp. sea salt
- 30 drops liquid stevia

CHOCOLATE TOPPING

- ¼ cup unsweetened organic cocoa powder (24 g)
- 2 Tbsp. coconut oil
- 2 Tbsp. erythritol (28 g)

KETO *Desserts*

DIRECTIONS

1. Line a 9x5" loaf pan with unbleached parchment paper.

2. In a small sauce pan over medium-low heat, melt almond butter and coconut oil. Stir in almond milk, sea salt and liquid stevia.

3. Add mixture to a blender or use an immersion blender to fully incorporate.

4. Pour into the lined pan. Refrigerate for 2 hours.

5. Make the chocolate topping. Melt the coconut oil and whisk in cocoa powder and erythritol. Drizzle over almond butter fudge. Cool for 10 minutes.

6. Place in the refrigerator to chill, until set. Slice into squares.

NUTRITION INFORMATION

314 calories, 33 g fat, 19 g saturated fat, 10 g monounsaturated fat, 3 g polyunsaturated fat, 5 mg cholesterol, 7 g carbohydrate, 4 g NET carbs, 2 g sugar alcohols, 1 g sugar, 1 g fiber, 4 g protein, 193 mg potassium, 123 mg phosphorous, 136 mg sodium, 72 mg magnesium

MACRONUTRIENT RATIO

91% FAT ■ 4% PROTEIN ■ 5% CARBOHYDRATE

KETO SALTED ALMOND BRITTLE

With its rich, buttery flavor and crisp, sweet snap, you'll love this quick, keto-friendly version of the classic Southern treat.

YIELD: 8 servings

INGREDIENTS

- ¼ cup butter (or palm shortening for dairy free)
- ½ cup erythritol, powdered (100 g)
- 2 tsp. vanilla
- ¼ tsp. sea salt
- 1 cup almonds
- ⅛ tsp. coarse sea salt

DIRECTIONS

1. Cut a piece of unbleached parchment paper to fit a round 9" pie pan or a 9x9" cake pan.

2. Melt butter in a small sauce pan on medium heat. Add erythritol, vanilla and sea salt. Stir until incorporated.

3. Add almonds and continue to stir until the mixture begins to bubble.

4. Continue stirring for another 2-3 minutes or until mixture becomes light brown.

5. Carefully pour on top of the lined baking pan and spread evenly.

6. Sprinkle coarse sea salt evenly across the top. Set aside to cool for 1 hour.

7. Once hardened, break into pieces.

NUTRITION INFORMATION

157 calories, 15g fat, 4 g saturated fat, 7 g monounsaturated fat, 2 g polyunsaturated fat, 15 mg cholesterol, 16g carbohydrate, 2 g NET carbs, 12 g sugar alcohols, 1 g sugar, 2 g fiber, 4 g protein, 129 mg potassium, 88 mg phosphorous, 114 mg sodium, 48 mg magnesium

MACRONUTRIENT RATIO

85% FAT ■ 10% PROTEIN ■ 5% CARBOHYDRATE

KETO ROLO

If you crave the crisp, chocolate shell and gooey, caramel center of a Rolo, you'll love our keto version of this classic candy.

YIELD: 12 candies

INGREDIENTS

CHOCOLATE SHELL

- 1 oz. *Lily's Chocolate Chips*
- 2 oz. cocoa butter
- 20 drops toffee-flavored liquid stevia
- ⅛ tsp. sea salt

CARAMEL FILLING

- 3 Tbsp. grass-fed butter
- 3 Tbsp. erythritol, powdered
- 1 Tbsp. organic heavy cream
- 1 Tbsp. coconut palm sugar
- ½ tsp. xanthan gum

DIRECTIONS

1. Add 1 inch of water to a double boiler or small saucepan with a stainless steel bowl on top. Bring to a boil.

2. Add cocoa butter and chocolate chips. Stir until melted. Turn heat off and stir in stevia and sea salt.

3. Carefully spoon chocolate into a truffle mold. Fill ⅓ full and ensure there is chocolate on all sides. Reserve about ¼ of the chocolate for topping.

4. Place in the freezer for 10 minutes to set.

5. Make the caramel filling. Melt butter in a small saucepan on medium-high heat. Add the erythritol, cream, coconut sugar and xanthan gum. Whisk the mixture until the caramel begins to bubble and darken (about 2 minutes).

6. Spoon caramel over chocolate in each candy mold. Return to freezer for 10 minutes.

7. Top each mold with remaining chocolate. Return to the freezer to set for an additional 10 minutes.

NUTRITION INFORMATION

83 calories, 9 g fat, 5 g saturated fat, 1 g monounsaturated fat, 0 g polyunsaturated fat, 9 mg cholesterol, 6 g carbohydrate, 1 g NET carbs, 4 g sugar alcohols, 1 g sugar, 1 g fiber, 0 g protein, 3 mg potassium, 2 mg phosphorous, 46 mg sodium, 0 mg magnesium

MACRONUTRIENT RATIO

93% FAT ■ 1% PROTEIN ■ 6% CARBOHYDRATE

Ice Creams

KETO MINT CHOCOLATE CHIP ICE CREAM

This cool and creamy ice cream with dark chocolate chips tops expensive low-sugar brands in both taste and texture. Feel free to swap coconut milk for the heavy cream to make it dairy free (and still ketogenic)!

YIELD: 1 pint (6 servings)

INGREDIENTS

- ¼ cup erythritol (42 g)
- 1 Tbsp. sunflower lecithin
- 4 Tbsp. MCT oil
- 1 tsp. organic peppermint extract
- 2 ounces *Lily's Dark Chocolate Chips*
- 2 cups organic heavy cream
- 2 Tbsp. grass-fed butter

DIRECTIONS

1. Powder the erythritol and sunflower lecithin. Make sure your ice cream maker is fully frozen.

2. In a medium saucepan, melt the butter. Add the cream and the erythritol-lecithin mixture, whisking well. Bring to a boil. Add the MCT oil and peppermint extract and whisk again. Let mixture cool.

3. Pour cream mixture into a blender. Holding the lid on tight, blend on high for 30 seconds. This aerates the mixture and provides a creamier result.

4. Pour cream mixture into ice cream maker. Freeze according to manufacturer's instructions. For best results, remove when ice cream is a thick, soft-serve consistency. Allowing the ice cream to over-freeze in the vessel changes the texture.

5. Fold in chocolate chips and transfer to a pint container. Freeze.

6. Soften on counter for 15-30 minutes or microwave in 10 second bursts to soften before serving.

NUTRITION INFORMATION

444 calories, 46 g fat, 32 g saturated fat, 10 g monounsaturated fat, 2 g polyunsaturated fat, 119 mg cholesterol, 14g carbohydrate, 4 g NET carbs, 8 g sugar alcohols, 0 g sugar, 3 g fiber, 2 g protein, 72 mg potassium, 50 mg phosphorous, 57 mg sodium, 6 mg magnesium

MACRONUTRIENT RATIO

95% FAT ■ 2% PROTEIN ■ 3% CARBOHYDRATE

KETO CHOCOLATE ICE CREAM

This uber-chocolatey ice cream boasts the silky texture of the original... without dairy! Add almond extract or chopped almonds for a unique twist.

YIELD: 1 pint (6 servings)

INGREDIENTS

- ¼ cup erythritol (42 g)
- 1 Tbsp. sunflower lecithin
- 3 Tbsp. organic cocoa powder
- 2 Tbsp. virgin coconut oil
- 2 cups coconut milk
- 1 pinch sea salt
- 1 tsp. vanilla extract
- 4 Tbsp. MCT oil
- 20 drops liquid stevia

DIRECTIONS

1. Powder the erythritol, cocoa powder and sunflower lecithin. Make sure your ice cream maker is fully frozen.

2. In a medium saucepan, melt the coconut oil. Add the coconut milk, vanilla extract, sea salt and the erythritol-lecithin-cocoa mixture, whisking well. Bring to a boil. Add the MCT oil and stevia and whisk again. Adjust sweetness. Let mixture cool.

3. Pour cream mixture into a blender. Holding the lid on tight, blend on high for 30 seconds. This aerates the mixture and provides a creamier result.

4. Pour cream mixture into ice cream maker. Freeze according to manufacturer's instructions. For best results, remove when ice cream is a thick, soft-serve consistency. Allowing the ice cream to over-freeze in the vessel changes the texture.

5. Transfer to a pint container and freeze.

6. Soften on counter for 15-30 minutes or microwave in 10 second bursts to soften before serving.

NUTRITION INFORMATION

296 calories, 31 g fat, 28 g saturated fat, 1 g monounsaturated fat, 1 g polyunsaturated fat, 0 mg cholesterol, 10 g carbohydrate, 3 g NET carbs, 6 g sugar alcohols, 0.1 g sugar, 1 g fiber, 2 g protein, 216 mg potassium, 91 mg phosphorous, 23 mg sodium, 47 mg magnesium

MACRONUTRIENT RATIO

95% FAT ■ 3% PROTEIN ■ 4% CARBOHYDRATE

KETO VANILLA BEAN ICE CREAM

The classic ice cream gets a low sugar, high-flavor makeover with real vanilla bean and grass-fed butter.

YIELD: 1 pint (6 servings)

INGREDIENTS

- ¼ cup erythritol (42 g)
- 1 Tbsp. sunflower lecithin
- 4 Tbsp. MCT oil
- 2 cups organic heavy cream
- 2 Tbsp. grass-fed butter
- 1 whole vanilla bean, scraped

DIRECTIONS

1. Powder the erythritol and sunflower lecithin. Make sure your ice cream maker is fully frozen.

2. In a medium saucepan, melt the butter. Add the cream, scraped vanilla bean and vanilla bean pod, and the erythritol-lecithin mixture, whisking well. Bring to a boil. Add the MCT oil and whisk again. Remove vanilla bean pod. Let mixture cool.

3. Pour cream mixture into a blender. Holding the lid on tight, blend on high for 30 seconds. This aerates the mixture and provides a creamier result.

4. Pour cream mixture into ice cream maker. Freeze according to manufacturer's instructions. For best results, remove when ice cream is a thick, soft-serve consistency. Allowing the ice cream to over-freeze in the vessel changes the texture.

5. Transfer to a pint container and freeze.

6. Soften on counter for 15-30 minutes or microwave in 10 second bursts to soften before serving.

NUTRITION INFORMATION

411 calories, 43 g fat, 30 g saturated fat, 10 g monounsaturated fat, 2 g polyunsaturated fat, 119 mg cholesterol, 8 g carbohydrate, 2 g NET carbs, 2 g sugar alcohols, 0.2 g sugar, 0 g fiber, 2 g protein, 74 mg potassium, 50 mg phosphorous, 57 mg sodium, 6 mg magnesium

MACRONUTRIENT RATIO

96% FAT ■ 2% PROTEIN ■ 2% CARBOHYDRATE

KETO BUTTER PECAN ICE CREAM

If you love this Southern-style ice cream flavor, you'll swoon for our rich, buttery keto version. For a twist on Pralines and Cream, add chopped Keto Salted Almond Brittle in lieu of the pecans.

YIELD: 6 servings

INGREDIENTS

- ¼ cup erythritol (42 g)
- 1 Tbsp. sunflower lecithin
- 4 Tbsp. MCT oil
- 2 cups organic heavy cream
- 2 Tbsp. grass-fed butter
- 1 tsp. vanilla extract
- ½ cup pecans, roughly chopped

DIRECTIONS

1. Powder the erythritol and sunflower lecithin. Make sure your ice cream maker is fully frozen.

2. In a medium saucepan, melt the butter. Add the pecans and cook over low heat, stirring for 5 minutes. Use a slotted spoon to remove the pecans and reserve.

3. Pour in the cream and the erythritol-lecithin mixture, whisking well. Bring to a boil. Add the MCT oil and vanilla extract and whisk again. Let mixture cool.

4. Pour cream mixture into blender. Holding the lid on tight, blend on high for 30 seconds. This aerates the mixture and provides a creamier result.

5. Pour cream mixture into ice cream maker. Freeze according to manufacturer's instructions. For best results, remove when ice cream is a thick, soft-serve consistency. Allowing the ice cream to over-freeze in the vessel changes the texture.

6. Transfer to a pint container and freeze.

7. Soften on counter for 15-30 minutes or microwave in 10 second bursts to soften before serving.

NUTRITION INFORMATION

467 calories, 49g fat, 31 g saturated fat, 13 g monounsaturated fat, 3 g polyunsaturated fat, 119 mg cholesterol, 9g carbohydrate, 3 g NET carbs, 6 g sugar alcohols, 1 g sugar, 1 g fiber, 2 g protein, 107 mg potassium, 73 mg phosphorous, 57 mg sodium, 16 mg magnesium

MACRONUTRIENT RATIO

96% FAT ■ 2% PROTEIN ■ 2% CARBOHYDRATE

Frostings & Toppings

COCOA BUTTER GANACHE

This melt-in-your-mouth topping creates an elegant presentation and adds rich chocolate flavor to classic layer cakes. Transform it into a fluffy frosting by chilling and whipping with pastured butter.

YIELD: 24 servings (Lightly glazes two 9" cakes)

INGREDIENTS

- 5 Tbsp. cocoa butter (75 g)
- 2 oz. organic baking chocolate
- 2 oz. dark chocolate (80% or higher)
- 1 Tbsp. vanilla extract
- 30 drops liquid stevia

DIRECTIONS

1. Roughly chop the cocoa butter and chocolates.

2. In a medium saucepan, melt the cocoa butter. Remove from heat. Add chocolate and stir to combine.

3. When all the chocolate has melted, add the vanilla and stevia, stirring well with a wooden spoon.

4. Let cool slightly before pouring over cake.

NUTRITION INFORMATION

49 calories, 5 g fat, 3 g saturated fat, 0.3 g monounsaturated fat, 0 g polyunsaturated fat, 0 mg cholesterol, 1 g carbohydrate, 1 g NET carbs, 0 g sugar alcohols, 0.4 g sugar, 1 g fiber, 1 g protein, 18 mg potassium, 8 mg phosphorous, 1 mg sodium, 7 mg magnesium

MACRONUTRIENT RATIO

90% FAT ■ 4% PROTEIN ■ 6% CARBOHYDRATE

LOW-CARB CARAMEL

Who doesn't love caramel? Our version of this gooey candy creation has just two net carbs per serving. Drizzle over Keto Brownies or Ice Cream for an over-the-top treat.

YIELD: 8 servings (1 Tbsp. each)

INGREDIENTS

- 3 Tbsp. grass-fed butter or palm shortening
- 3 Tbsp. erythritol
- 1 Tbsp. coconut sugar
- ½ Tbsp. coconut milk
- 1 tsp. xanthan gum (optional, for "stretch")

DIRECTIONS

1. In a medium saucepan, melt the butter or shortening over low heat.

2. Add the erythritol and coconut sugar. Whisk to combine. Add coconut milk and xanthan gum.

3. Continue whisking over heat for 2 minutes, letting caramel bubble and darken.

4. Drizzle warm caramel over brownies or ice cream. Store remainder in an airtight container. Microwave in 15 second bursts to soften, melt and use again.

NUTRITION INFORMATION

45 calories, 4 g fat, 3 g saturated fat, 1 g monounsaturated fat, 0.2 g polyunsaturated fat, 11 mg cholesterol, 6 g carbohydrate, 2 g NET carbs, 5 g sugar alcohols, 2 g sugar, 0.1 g fiber, 0.1 g protein, 3 mg potassium, 1 mg phosphorous, 33 mg sodium, 0.1 mg magnesium

MACRONUTRIENT RATIO

86% FAT ■ 1% PROTEIN ■ 13% CARBOHYDRATE

KETO CHOCOLATE BUTTERCREAM

Whether you prefer spreading it over classic Yellow or Chocolate Cake, our version of chocolate buttercream is just as rich and delicious as the sugar-filled original.

YIELD: 24 servings (Covers two-8" cakes)

INGREDIENTS

- 10 Tbsp. grass-fed butter or palm shortening (room temp)
- ¼ cup erythritol, powdered very fine (50 g)
- ⅓ cup cocoa powder, sifted (33 g)
- 2 Tbsp. coconut milk or organic heavy cream
- 1 tsp. vanilla extract
- 1 pinch sea salt
- ½ tsp. liquid stevia

DIRECTIONS

1. In a medium bowl, add the butter (or shortening) and erythritol. Using a hand-held mixer, beat on medium for 2 minutes to cream.

2. Add sifted cocoa powder, a little at a time, blending well.

3. Add coconut milk (or heavy cream), vanilla, sea salt and stevia. Beat on medium-high for 1 minute or until completely smooth.

4. Spread over cakes.

NUTRITION INFORMATION

47 calories, 5 g fat, 3 g saturated fat, 1 g monounsaturated fat, 0.2 g polyunsaturated fat, 13 mg cholesterol, 3 g carbohydrate, 0.3 g NET carbs, 2 g sugar alcohols, 0.1 g sugar, 0.4 g fiber, 0.3 g protein, 18 mg potassium, 9 mg phosphorous, 40 mg sodium, 5 mg magnesium

MACRONUTRIENT RATIO

96% FAT ■ 2% PROTEIN ■ 2% CARBOHYDRATE

KETO GERMAN CHOCOLATE FROSTING

The irresistible combination of coconut, pecans and chocolate – now sugar free and ketogenic!

YIELD: 24 servings (Covers two 8" cakes)

INGREDIENTS

- ½ cup organic full fat coconut milk
- ¼ cup erythritol, powdered (50 g)
- 2 large pastured egg yolks
- 4 Tbsp. organic virgin coconut oil
- 30 drops liquid stevia
- ½ tsp. vanilla extract
- 2 ounces organic coconut flakes, unsweetened (56 g)
- 1 cup organic pecans, chopped

DIRECTIONS

1. In a large saucepan, combine coconut milk, erythritol, egg yolks, coconut oil, stevia and vanilla.

2. Cook over low heat, stirring constantly, until thick.

3. Remove from heat and stir in pecans and coconut.

4. Spread on cake while still warm.

NUTRITION INFORMATION

78 calories, 8 g fat, 5 g saturated fat, 2 g monounsaturated fat, 1 g polyunsaturated fat, 17 mg cholesterol, 3 g carbohydrate, 1 g NET carbs, 2 g sugar alcohols, 0.4 g sugar, 1 g fiber, 1 g protein, 42 mg potassium, 26 mg phosphorous, 2 mg sodium, 9 mg magnesium

MACRONUTRIENT RATIO

93% FAT ■ 4% PROTEIN ■ 3% CARBOHYDRATE

0 NET CARBS | **DAIRY FREE** | **PALEO FRIENDLY**

KETO VANILLA BUTTERCREAM FROSTING

This classic buttercream lends itself to cakes of all kinds. To punch up the vanilla flavor without affecting the buttery hue, try vanilla-flavored liquid stevia.

YIELD: 12 servings (Covers one 8" cake)

INGREDIENTS

- 4 Tbsp. coconut oil
- 4 Tbsp. grass-fed butter or palm shortening
- 20-30 drops liquid stevia (vanilla flavor preferred)
- ½ tsp. arrowroot starch
- ½ tsp. vanilla extract

DIRECTIONS

1. In a medium bowl, add the coconut oil, butter (or shortening), vanilla and stevia.

2. Using a hand-held mixer, beat on medium for 2 minutes to cream.

3. Add the arrowroot starch, a little at a time, while continuing to blend on low speed. Frosting will thicken.

4. Spread over cooled cake.

NUTRITION INFORMATION

74 calories, 8 g fat, 6 g saturated fat, 1 g monounsaturated fat, 0 g polyunsaturated fat, 10 mg cholesterol, 0 g carbohydrate, 0 g NET carbs, 0 g sugar alcohols, 0 g sugar, 0 g fiber, 0 g protein, 1 mg potassium, 1 mg phosphorous, 27 mg sodium, 0 mg magnesium

MACRONUTRIENT RATIO

100% FAT ■ 0% PROTEIN ■ 0% CARBOHYDRATE

KETO CREAM CHEESE FROSTING

Perfect slathered on red velvet or carrot cake. For a dairy-free version, use Kite Hill brand Cream Cheese Style Spread.

YIELD: 24 servings (Covers two 8" cakes)

INGREDIENTS

- 8 oz. organic cream cheese (room temp)
- 2 Tbsp. grass-fed butter or palm shortening (room temp)
- 3 Tbsp. erythritol, powdered very fine
- 1 Tbsp. coconut milk or organic heavy cream
- 1 tsp. vanilla extract
- ½ tsp. liquid stevia

DIRECTIONS

1. In a medium bowl, add the cream cheese, butter or shortening and erythritol. Using a hand-held mixer, beat on medium for 2 minutes to cream.

2. Add coconut milk or heavy cream, vanilla and stevia. Beat on medium-high for 1 minute or until completely smooth.

3. Spread over cooled cake.

NUTRITION INFORMATION

85 calories, 9 g fat, 5 g saturated fat, 2 g monounsaturated fat, 0.3 g polyunsaturated fat, 26 mg cholesterol, 4 g carbohydrate, 1 g NET carbs, 3 g sugar alcohols, 0.1 g sugar, 0 g fiber, 1 g protein, 23 mg potassium, 20 mg phosphorous, 69 mg sodium, 1 mg magnesium

MACRONUTRIENT RATIO

91% FAT ■ 7% PROTEIN ■ 3% CARBOHYDRATE

SUGAR-FREE ORANGE MARMALADE

Most store-bought versions of this classic are loaded with sugar or artificial sweeteners. Our sugar-free version is bursting with orange flavor that compliments cookies, cakes, biscuits, breads and more!

YIELD: 12 servings (1 Tbsp. each)

INGREDIENTS

- 6 organic mandarin orange peels, finely sliced and diced
- 2 organic orange peels, finely sliced and diced
- 7 Tbsp. erythritol (84 g)
- 1 Tbsp. lemon juice
- 2 tsp. grass-fed gelatin
- ¾ tsp. liquid stevia extract (to taste)

DIRECTIONS

1. Place the orange peels in a pot. Cover with water and bring to a boil. Strain, discard the water and repeat.

2. Using a sharp knife or a food processor, dice or pulse the orange peel to very fine bits.

3. Return diced peel to pot and pour in just enough water to cover. Bring to a boil.

4. Reduce heat to a simmer. Add the erythritol and lemon juice. Simmer 15 minutes.

5. Add 2 Tbsp. water to a small bowl. Sprinkle gelatin over the top. Let stand 5 min to bloom.

6. Peels should now be soft. Remove from heat, let cool 5 minutes. Stir in bloomed gelatin and stevia.

7. Pour into a glass jar with a tight fitting lid. Let marmalade come to room temperature before refrigerating.

NUTRITION INFORMATION

7 calories, 0 g fat, 0 g saturated fat, 0 g monounsaturated fat, 0 g polyunsaturated fat, 0 mg cholesterol, 8 g carbohydrate, 1 g NET carbs, 6 g sugar alcohols, 0 g sugar, 1 g fiber, 0.4 g protein, 13 mg potassium, 1 mg phosphorous, 1 mg sodium, 1 mg magnesium

MACRONUTRIENT RATIO

2% FAT ■ 29% PROTEIN ■ 69% CARBOHYDRATE

COCONUT WHIPPED CREAM

This quick and healthy dairy-free alternative to traditional whipped cream is simple to make. Add ½ tsp. vanilla extract or lemon extract for a flavorful twist.

YIELD: 2 cups (16 servings of 2 Tbsp. each)

INGREDIENTS

- 1 can coconut milk (13½ oz.)
- 15 drops liquid stevia (to taste)

DIRECTIONS

1. Place the can of coconut milk in the refrigerator and chill overnight.

2. Place a medium-sized, deep metal mixing bowl and beaters in the freezer.

3. Remove coconut milk from refrigerator, but do not agitate (you want it to remain separated). Open the can and scoop off the cream layer that has risen to the top.

4. Place cream in chilled bowl. Beat the coconut cream on high speed for 2-3 minutes or until fluffy peaks form.

5. Add stevia drops while mixing to incorporate.

NUTRITION INFORMATION

23 calories, 3 g fat, 2 g saturated fat, 0 g monounsaturated fat, 0 g polyunsaturated fat, 0 mg cholesterol, 0.4 g carbohydrate, 0.4 g NET carbs, 0 g sugar alcohols, 0.4 g sugar, 0 g fiber, 0.2 g protein, 0 mg potassium, 0 mg phosphorous, 6 mg sodium, 0 mg magnesium

MACRONUTRIENT RATIO

91% FAT ■ 3% PROTEIN ■ 6% CARBOHYDRATE

SUGAR-FREE LEMON GLAZE

The crowning touch on spice cakes and pound cakes, this bright and fresh sugar-free glaze is super simple to make.

YIELD: 16 servings

INGREDIENTS

- ½ cup erythritol, powdered (100 g)
- 2 tsp. lemon juice

DIRECTIONS

1. In a small bowl, whisk powdered erythritol and lemon juice together.

2. The glaze should be thick, but pourable. If glaze is too thick, add water in ¼ tsp. increments until a thick, pourable consistency is reached.

3. Spread over cake and allow some to drip down sides.

4. Let sit for 15 minutes then serve.

NUTRITION INFORMATION

0 calories, 0 g fat, 0 g saturated fat, 0 g monounsaturated fat, 0 g polyunsaturated fat, 0 mg cholesterol, 6 g carbohydrate, 0 g NET carbs, 6 g sugar alcohols, 0.4 g sugar, 0 g fiber, 0 g protein, 0 mg potassium, 0 mg phosphorous, 0 mg sodium, 0 mg magnesium

MACRONUTRIENT RATIO

0% FAT ■ 0% PROTEIN ■ 100% CARBOHYDRATE

KETO MAGIC SHELL

The addictively delicious, freeze-on-contact ice cream topping of the 1980s is back... and now with real food ingredients and zero sugar!

YIELD: 16 servings

INGREDIENTS

- 6 Tbsp. virgin coconut oil
- 6 Tbsp. organic cocoa powder
- 20 drops liquid stevia
- 1 pinch sea salt

DIRECTIONS

1. In a small saucepan, melt coconut oil.

2. Stir in cocoa, salt and stevia, whisking well.

3. Let cool slightly, and then pour over homemade keto ice cream.

4. Store in covered container in the refrigerator. Reheat in the microwave in 10 second bursts.

NUTRITION INFORMATION

50 calories, 6g fat, 5 g saturated fat, 0.4 g monounsaturated fat, 0.1 g polyunsaturated fat, 0 mg cholesterol, 1 g carbohydrate, 0.4 g NET carbs, 0 g sugar alcohols, 0 g sugar, 1 g fiber, 0.4 g protein, 29 mg potassium, 14 mg phosphorous, 5 mg sodium, 9 mg magnesium

MACRONUTRIENT RATIO

94% FAT ■ 3% PROTEIN ■ 3% CARBOHYDRATE